a century in
CHARLESTON

A family history
by
Aryeh Wetherhorn

ISBN 978-965-92747-2-7
First edition - November 2022
published by Aryeh Wetherhorn

Foreword

This is the place where I thank all the family members who helped by sending me anecdotes and material. This is a process that has been going on for years. I won't mention names here. I mentioned privacy issues in the introduction. I will tell you that I'm solely responsible for any errors that might have crept in. The only person that gets mentioned by name is Talya Shachar-Albocher. She did the layout and got the finished product together. She also did the covers, front and back, and would have done any artwork other than photos and news clippings if any had been included. Thank you, Talya.

Introduction

When I was in high school I was often curious about my father's family. My mother's family was very close, and we often met, even though we lived far apart. This wasn't the case with my father. His parents died when he was younger. When I asked about them I was told, among other things, that my great grandfather had been a civil war general in the confederate forces. One of my cousins had a book that mentioned this. Well, it wasn't entirely true. But I didn't know that at the time. I started reading every book I could lay my hands on in order to find a General Wetherhorn.

What I discovered then, and afterwards, is the basis for this book. I've separated it into chapters about each of the principal family members. Each chapter starts with a short family tree. If a family member has a separate chapter of his own, only the fact of his birth may be mentioned in the chapter devoted to his parents. Anything about someone who never married or raised a family is usually included in the chapter about his or her parents. Chapters are numbered according to their chronological appearance in the trees. The first chapters got sequential numbers. Their descendants got the same number, but with a letter added. The next generation followed the same pattern by adding an additional number. I follow the genealogy approach and mention the major life events; Birth, Marriage, Divorce (when applicable) and Death. But in between I include additional specific items I discovered pertaining to the individual, and descriptions of other events and features that help illuminate the time when they lived.

The adventure of seeking family roots took me many places. It put me in contact with many distant relatives, some of whom I have still not met face to face. I decided to cut off the family story in 1940. That means I have inter-faith marriages between Jews and Christians (mostly Catholic), but don't include later inter-racial marriages between Wetherhorn descendants and African-Americans, Japanese,

Chinese, and Koreans. The 1940 cutoff is also important because it helps me to avoid writing about many people who are still alive today. Privacy is important. The sources I've consulted are almost all readily avail- able to anyone who does genealogical research. I'd like to think that I went a bit deeper than most genealogists. There were often items that seemed contradictory, like 2 siblings listed as being born less than nine months apart in different sources. Even the family name was a problem. But that story will be the subject of one of the chapters. I hope you find it both entertaining and enriching.

A Century in Charleston

Contents

Marcus Wetherhorn
1812-1873

Spouse	**Tsippora Esther**
Children	Philip Wetherhorn p. 20
	Solomon Wetherhorn p. 62
	Levy Wetherhorn p. 100
	Abraham Wetherhorn p. 27
	Henry Wetherhorn p. 156
Spouse	**Bertha Zacharias**
Children	Sigmund Wetherhorn p. 170
	Annie Wetherhorn p. 174
	Solomon Wetherhorn
	David B. Wetherhorn p. 80

1

Marcus Wetherhorn

When someone mentions the year 1812 what comes to mind? Some will think of it as the year the infant United States fought a second war for independence against Great Britain. Others will remember it as the year Napoleon invaded Russia. A few will think of Tchaikovsky's classic "1812 Overture", inspired by Napoleon's invasion. For me, it was the year my great-great-grandfather was born. Malchus Wetterhahn was born on February 12th in Holzheim. It was a tiny village in the German province of Hesse, about 50 kilometers North of Frankfurt. The Wetterhahn family was just one of many Jewish families in the village. I know nothing about his parents, Biehle (nee Schawes) and Feitel Uri, His birth was statistically insignificant in a total world population that numbered just under a billion people. In the 21st century both China and India have populations greater than that of the entire planet in 1812.

Almost 6 years earlier Napoleon had convened his 'Great Sanhedrin' in Paris to help him integrate Jews into the fabric of French society. The directorate of the French Republic that ruled France after the French Revolution had given French Jews citizenship in 1791. But citizenship by decree doesn't mean that the ideals of Liberty, Equality, and Fraternity had actually been extended to Jews in practice. The ideals of the revolution were extended to all the territories that Napoleon conquered after he came to power. Equality and integration seemed to be forgotten after Napoleon was defeated. But despite the image of peace in Europe that followed, there were still local conflicts. Unrest and discrimination may have been contributing factors in the decision Malchus made. His father had died in 1828. He, his wife, Tsippora, whom he had married in 1830, and his two young sons, Philip, age 4 and new- born infant Solomon, left Holzheim to go to America.

For whatever reasons, Malchus, or Marcus, as he was subsequently known in English, went from Germany to Charleston, South Carolina in 1840-41 with his family. They probably went directly, rather than via some other port of entry. At that time immigration was handled by the individual states. The US Federal government didn't begin to control immigration until 1890. The Ellis Island terminal in New York only went into operation in 1897.Also, Charleston had a large Jewish community, even larger than that of New York at the time. In addition it had a large German community. A common national background and language was often even more important than a common religion in those days. The crossing from Europe might have been in a sailing ship. The first regularly scheduled steamship crossings had only begun in 1838. Sailing ships continued to carry both freight and passengers for a few more decades before being replaced by the faster and more economical steam powered ships.

The family name, Wetterhahn, underwent a typical American transformation. The meeting of the German accented Wetterhahn with the English spoken in the Southern United States resulted in a near phonetic equivalent spelled Wetherhorn. There would be many other phonetic, or near phonetic spellings by people over the years to come. Marcus earned his living by selling clothing .According to a footnote on page 304 of the records for Charleston, vol. 7 in the R. G. Dun & Co. Collection at the Baker Library of the Harvard Business School he took a small loan from a financing service in New York, and went into partnership with another German immigrant named Zacharias. They sold ready to wear clothing to some of the poorer residents of Charleston. His partner died and Marcus apparently went bankrupt just prior to the American Civil War. But that last item might not be completely accurate. The Charleston City Directory for 1859, the year he reportedly was bankrupt, shows him with a clothing store of King Street, be- low Cannon Street, and living upstairs from the shop. The 1861 City census book has him renting a brick house belonging to Philip McBride at 502 King Street. McBride owned an entire row of 9 houses, some brick and some wood, on that street. A later City Directory, from 1867, lists him with a clothing store at 615 King Street. The numbering system wasn't always consistent, but 629 King Street was the first house above Cannon in one of the numbering guides.

The Wetherhorns joined the existing Jewish congregation of Kehilat Kodesh Beth Elohim (KKBE). The translation of the Hebrew name is "The Holy Congregation of the House of the Lord". KKBE was just moving in to a new building. The older synagogue had been destroyed in a major city fire in April, 1838 that burned down about a third of the entire city. KKBE had been founded by Sephardic Jews in 1749. It was the 4th oldest Jewish congregation in America. The building, constructed in 1840, is still standing and has been recognized as a National Historic Landmark. It is the 2nd oldest Jewish house of worship in the US today, and the oldest to have been in continuous use since it was constructed. Along with the new building came some important changes in ritual. The congregation had survived a serious split when newer immigrants asked for more English in the service, including the Rabbi's sermon. The sermon had been given in Ladino, a form of Judeo-Spanish. The newer arrivals tended to speak Yiddish, a form of Judeo-German and followed the Ashkenazic ritual rather than the Sephardic that was originally used at KKBE. The first request for change was made around 1824 was rejected, but by 1840 conditions were different. The ritual was not only liberalized, but an organ was installed in the building in a balcony at the back of the sanctuary. Strict Orthodox Jewish observance today does not allow playing ANY musical instrument on the Sabbath. The more traditional members were upset. KKBE also had a choir, and used the organ to accompany them. It was probably one of the first steps toward the creation of the Reform Jewish Movement in America. When the Union of Reform Judaism was formally organized in 1873 KKBE was a proud founding member congregation.

The Ashkenazic traditionalists finally broke away in 1854 and formed their own congregation, Brith Shalom (Covenant of Peace). It later amalgamated with another group, Beth Israel (The House of Israel) to form todays BSBI which is the oldest Modern Orthodox Jewish Congregation in the Southern United States. Philip- Wetherhorn, the oldest son on Marcus and Tsippora, would later join Brith Shalom.

Tsippora, who was known in English as Sophie, was a couple of years older than Marcus. She had three more children in Charleston. Levy was the first to be born in the new world, in 1842. Abraham Andrew followed in 1844 and Henry in 1847.

The U.S. Census of 1850 has couple of interesting things that shed some more light on the early history of the Wetherhorns. To start with, they are listed as living in the Parish of St. Philip and St. Michaels. That title stems from the name of the first church erected in Charleston, St. Philips that was later replaced by another structure, St. Michaels. The church was located on the corner of Broad Street and Meeting Street. The city was divided into 2 Anglican parishes in 1751. The one North of Broad Street became St. Philips Parish while the area south of Broad Street became the new Parish of St. Michaels. For the 1850 census the area was referred to as the Parish of St. Philips and St. Michaels. On September 20th of 1850 census taker Morris Goldsmith visited the 73rd structure in the area of his responsibility. The Wetherhorn family was the 81st family he recorded. He listed Marcus as the head of the family and a shopkeeper. His wife, Sophia and their 5 boys followed. Then he listed Eliezer Cohen, a 50 year old peddler from Germany, living at the same address. This isn't a big surprise. Many families supplemented their incomes by taking in boarders. Mr. Cohen was probably among them. The 4 older children were all noted as having attended school. Henry, being only aged 3 at the time, wasn't included in that category.

The next item I noted shows one of the many problems you can encounter when looking at old, handwritten, records using modern scanning techniques. Number 2 son was named Solomon. But the census records him as Zalack. The automated scan changed that to "Lalack". The mistake came from a language problem. Marcus didn't read or write English. He dictated his will and it had to be translated and written in English. He then made an "X" mark, witnessed by others, in order to make it official. Solomon seems to have been called "Solick" in Yiddish. It's a very common diminutive. Census taker Goldsmith wrote it as "Zalack". A computer scan read the "Z" as an "L". The result was that several people doing genealogy research have copied and perpetuated the error many times.

Another item worth mentioning here is that the total population of Charleston in 1850 was 42,985. It was further broken down into 3 categories; 20,012 whites, 3,441

free coloreds, and 19,532 slaves. The Wetherhorns were never slave owners. But slavery was definitely part of the environment in which they lived.

Sophie died from Cholera in 1855. She was buried in the old Jewish Cemetery on Coming Street.

Marcus remarried in 1857. His New Wife, the former Bertha Zacharias, was much younger. She was just 27, or possibly even younger. He was 45. She, too, came from Germany. She had been in America only 3 years. Marcus continued to support his family as a clothing merchant, and they rented their home. It would be more accurate to say they rented a series of homes, because their address changes over the next few years. Bertha made a second family for Marcus. Her first son, Sigmund, was born in 1858. The first of the older boys were already leaving home by then. Annie was born in 1861, Solomon in 1862, and David in 1864.

It may have caught your attention that Marcus had 2 sons named Solomon, one with each wife. Ashkenazi (European) Jewish traditions include a policy of naming a newborn infant after someone who had previously died. In the case of the first Solomon Wetherhorn, Marcus probably knew he had left home and joined the Confederate Army during the American Civil War. He may have heard that Solomon had been killed. The first Solomon never returned to Charleston. So it would have been a reasonable assumption.

The US Census was important because it determines the allocation of seats in the US Congress. The 36th Congress was based on the 1850 Census. The Senate at that date had 66 members, and the House of Representatives would have 237. Six of them were from South Carolina. Both Senators and Congressmen received $6000 for each 2 year session, and in addition they were paid for travel to Washington, DC at the rate of $8 for every 20 miles between their homes and the capitol. Travel was paid for only once per session. By the end of December, 1860, the State of South Carolina had seceded from the Union and her senators and representatives resigned and returned home. The representative from the 2nd district, which included Charleston, was William Porcher Miles. He had previously been the Mayor of the city, Today, his major legacy is that he designed the flag that would become the battle flag of the Army of Virginia, and it is a frequent target for left wing movements claiming to be against racism.

The 1860 US Census included Marcus and his family. Philip had already moved out, and they had a 20 year old German house-keeper named Pauline Reddick.

The Civil War, or, The War between the States, as some prefer to call it, had a major impact on the Wetherhorn family. The 5 older boys all served with the military forces of the confederacy. Their individual stories will be covered in their own chapters. Marcus remained in Charleston with Bertha and their children. Many members of the Jewish community fled when the city was under siege and being bombarded from land and sea late in the war. KKBE even evacuated their Torah scrolls to Columbia.

The local government had approved plans for the creation of the Charleston City Railway before the war. Implementing those plans was delayed. But in December, 1866, Charleston got its' first mass transport system. The Charleston City Rail Company (CRCC) laid tracks down several major thoroughfares and used horse drawn cars to carry people from place to place. There were about a dozen cars in service. Each car had a capacity of 20-25 persons. The cars for the two separate lines were distinguished from one another by color. Service lasted until 10 PM.

The main route started from the old post office. A double set of tracks ran over Broad Street west to Meeting and north on Meeting to Calhoun Street and then across Calhoun one block to King Street. The tracks then went along King to the final station at Shepard Street. The King Street line used yellow cars and blue lights. There was also a single branch route that ran off of the main line at the corner of Meeting and Wentworth streets. It ran across Wentworth to Rutledge and up Rutledge to Spring Street. The Rutledge line used red cars and red lights. Cars going to the battery also carried red flags. Each line had 6 numbered cars.

When service started, in 1866, it was, de facto, segregated; there were no separate cars for blacks. The newly free former slaves were allowed to ride on the front and rear platforms, but not inside the tram cars. In March, 1866, following a black political rally, a few Negroes tried to board a tram and go inside. The conductor halted the vehicle and the men were arrested and removed by local police and federal soldiers. On April First two more blacks were detained after they had been warned not to go inside. This time there was a lot of crowd unrest that even resulted in a few injuries. This story came to head on April 17th, 1867 when Mary P. Bowers, a black woman, was denied entrance and forcibly put off one of the trams. She appealed to the Freedmen's Bureau Commissioner, a position created under the Federal Reconstruction Act. The Commissioner spoke with the heads of the City Railway. A compromise was reached. No formal rules were written, but blacks were accepted as regular, and equal, riders. That status continued in Charleston for over 30 years. I doubt that Rosa Parks, who instigated a similar protest in Montgomery, Alabama in 1965 ever heard of Mary Bowers, but they both made a serious contribution to the case for equality under the law.

The main post office was located on East Bay Street, opposite Broad Street. In 1888 there were 10 men employed as carriers for home delivery. Mail addressed by street and number was taken by carriers. Other items went to General Delivery. The General delivery office was open from 08:30 to 18:30 daily and on Sunday from 12:00 to 13:00. Items not called for were advertised in the largest circulation newspaper on Friday of each week. To claim such an item one had to give one's full name and the date of the advertisement. If it remained unclaimed for a month the item was forwarded to the dead letter office in Washington, DC.

On February 15th, 1873 Marcus made a last will which was filed with the Charleston Probate Court. It was witnessed by Asher D. Cohen, an attorney who had offices at 330 King Street and who probably also wrote it in English. Marcus's English was very likely not that good. Marcus died on February 26th 1873 in Charleston and was buried in the Coming Street Jewish Cemetery.

His second wife, Bertha, remained in Charleston for a while longer. In 1880 she was living in St. Matthews with all of her 4 children.

Annie and Sigmund, have chapters of their own. Solomon and David, neither of whom ever married, are included with Sigmund.

Bertha stayed with her daughter Annie's family in St. Matthews until she, too, died, on June 19th, 1915.

It seems to me that this is a good place to say something more about the old Jewish Cemetery on Coming Street. Today it is closed to the public. The entrance is locked. One has to make an appointment to visit. It is listed in the National Register of Historic places. That's because it is the oldest surviving Jewish Cemetery in the American South. It was later supplanted by the newer cemeteries on Huguenin Street, further to the north.

Inside the cemetery there are some 500 graves. A number of them are unmarked. The center of the cemetery is shaded by a very old, and very large, magnolia tree. The land was originally purchased by the DaCosta family in 1754 as a private burial ground. About ten years later they sold it to the KKBE congregation. When the Shearit Israel congregation split from KKBE they established their own cemetery alongside the older plot, and erected a high wall to mark the separation. That wall no longer exists. What remains is a low separation. But there is a fenced off section further east that marks where Catherine Hinton Lopez, the wife of David Lopez Jr., was buried in 1843. She had not formally converted to Judaism and the administrators refused to allow her to be interred in a Jewish Cemetery. Some of the markers have deteriorated over time. Without the record of the Elzas book about Jewish cemeteries I would have had a difficult time reading the inscription on Marcus Wetherhorn's grave.

Philip Wetherhorn 1836-1897	
Spouse	**Mina**
Children	Sophia Wetherhorn
Spouse	**Sarah**
Children	A Wetherhorn
	Isaac Wetherhorn

2
Philip Wetherhorn

Philip Wetherhorn was born on September 14th. 1836. I have often felt that Philip, who was the oldest child of Marcus and Tsippora, was sometimes a tragic figure. He went through a lot of difficult times when he was younger. It starts with him moving from his safe and secure home surroundings in 1840. He was just 4 years old when his parents took him to America. Steam powered ships were not all that common yet, so they probably came on a sailing ship. If it was anything like other accounts I've read, it meant days spent below decks in a relatively small space. A typical crossing of the Atlantic would often last several weeks. Then, on arrival, he found himself in the midst of a lot of strangers who spoke a language he did not understand. But children of that age are resilient, and I'm sure he overcame any difficulties.

The next major challenge came when his mother died in 1855. When his father remarried, it seems Philip had to go out and make his own way. According to US Army recruitment records a Philip Wetherhorn tried to enlist. The record says he signed up in New Haven on July 10th, 1857 for a 5 year term of service. It also notes he had grey eyes, dark complexion, was 5' 4 ½" tall and had been a clerk. It seems someone objected to the process because he was released on August 6th with the cryptic notation "By civil authority". I am not certain this record is referring to the same person. New Haven is a long way from Charleston. But after the civil war there was a move to record people for the Georgia State Militia. That record ALSO says that a Philip Wetherhorn was enrolled, and released. This time was with a different cryptic notation; "foreign rites".

Philip appears as Philip Wetherhahn in the 1859 Charleston city directory living 66 State Street and employed as an accountant at 171 East Bay St. The following year the entry has changed slightly, showing him as P. Wetterhorn, a bookkeeper

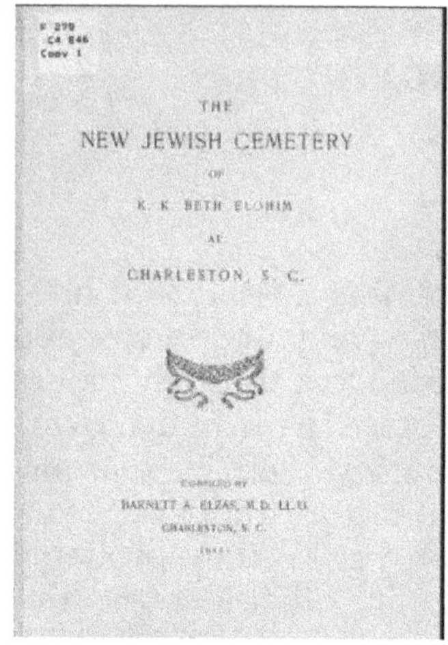

for Cadow, McKenzie & Co. and boarding at King St. near Horlbeck Alley. House numbers on streets from that era were not consistent. The numbering system went through more than one change before settling down to what they are now.

Philip married a young woman named Mina and they had one daughter together. The only evidence I found for this is page 7 of Dr. Barnett Elzas's book of KKBE gravestone inscriptions. According to that source, Mina appears to have died on July 19th, 1863 at the age of 19. Their daughter, Sophia, only lived for a total of 7 months and 3 days. She died on July 31st, 1863, which means she was born about December 28th, 1862.

In 1862 Philip was actually enlisted in the Confederate army. He appears as a private in Prendergast's company of the 16th SC militia regiment. The 16th was based in Charleston, and was similar to today's National Guard. His brother, Levy, also was briefly a member of this regiment. His story comes later. The 16th was mobilized by the state governor in December 1861 for 12 months service after South Carolina seceded. It isn't clear whether Philip was enrolled only for that period.

WETHERHORN, LEVI, B. June 13, 1842; D. Jan. 28, 1910.
WETHERHORN, MARCUS, son of L. and P. Wetherhorn, D. Mar. 30, 1892, Aet. 16 yrs. 1 m. 14 dys.
WETHERHORN, MINA, wife of P. Wetherhorn, D. July 19, 1863, Aet. 19.
WETHERHORN, SOPHIA, child of P. and Mina Wetherhorn, D. July 31, 1863, Aet. 7 mos. 3 dys.
WETHERHORN, SOPHIA, daughter of L. and P. Wetherhorn, D. Dec. 17, 1882, Aet. 15 yrs. 25 dys.

P. Wetherhorn is on the muster roll for this regiment. The original document in NARA M267 - #586957 (2 pages, microfilm?) available via footnote.com From civil war histories I found that the regiment was called up in December, 1861, for 12 months state service and assigned to Gen Albert S. Johnston's department in Charleston.

On April 28th, 1862, the unit was transferred to Confederate States national service for 3 years or the duration of the war. In May 1863 it was assigned to the Army of Tennessee and

marched off to relieve Vicksburg. It arrived too late to influence the campaign and returned to the East. The regiment missed the battle of Chickamauga but fought in delaying actions in February, 1864, all the way to Atlanta. I have no definite record that Philip was still with the regiment then. General Hood engaged General Sherman at Nashville and Franklin and the 16th SC regiment had 56 men killed in those actions. I next found him mentioned as living in Georgia and working as cigar maker in 1864. That was when the "foreign rites" story happened. But by the next year he was back in Charleston. In 1865 he married Sarah. Who was about 2 years younger than he was. She came to the US in 1858 from Germany. They had two children together. Philip and Sarah joined the Orthodox Ashkenazi congregation of Berith Shalome that had formed in 1854. It later became todays Brit Shalom Beth Israel (BSBI) and is the oldest Orthodox congregation in the American South. They probably affiliated with Berith Shalome after the Civil War because Philip's first wife and child were buried in the BS Cemetery, but Sarah was buried in the Magnolia Street Cemetery of BSBI.

Philip tried working as a shopkeeper. The March 1866 tax records shop that Philip was assessed $1.67 in Mount Pleasant He's listed along with 3 others, L Wagner, A. Winberg, and Henry Wolff. The four might have been partners in a Mount Pleasant retail shop. In any case, Philip went into business on his own by 1867. He had a variety store at 475 King Street. The Charleston Daily News, October 11, 1867, has a list of passengers on the steamer EMILY B SOUDER bound for New York. It includes P. Wetherhorn. He may have traveled north to secure funding for opening his own business, or for purchasing stock. The two children, sons Alexander and Isaac, were both born in Charleston. The former was born in 1866 and his brother in 1868. I have only one record of Isaac. He was reported to have died of a brain tumor in Montgomery, Alabama, in 1905. Alexander never married. He died in 1915 after several years of working as a clerk and bookkeeper in various businesses in Charleston. Meanwhile, Phillip decided to sell clothing. The new shop was located nearby, at 569 King Street. The family had a single 22 year old black house servant, Betsie Grant, in 1870. Betsie was not a slave, but she was illiterate. It seems she never did learn to read and write, but she did marry and had 9 children. Household servants were quite common in Charleston even after emancipation. It is interesting to note that while South Carolina was neither part of the Cotton Belt nor the most populous of the Confederate States, it had the highest proportion of slaves to free white citizens in the entire Confederacy at the start of the Civil War. Around 1910, when Sarah was a widow, she still employed a black male servant to help at home.

The new Wetherhorn business resulted in a couple of interesting adventures. The *Charleston Daily News* of June 01, 1871 reported that at 6 o'clock on Tuesday evening Philip returned to 569 King Street to find a colored youth hiding in the closet, waiting to ransack the home. The young man was turned over to the police.

The same newspaper reported on December 18th, 1871, that at about 11 o'clock Saturday night a young man of decent appearance entered the store of Mr. Wetherhorn on upper King St. and asked to see some coats. He selected one and asked for change for a large bill. When given the change he left the store wearing the coat and taking both the change and the original note. The proprietor shouted and pursued, to no avail. Police heard about it and the man was arrested.

Philip seems to have spent the next few years moving from one location to another, and even changing the type of store he operated. Here are a few dates:

1878 . . . . Dry goods store....................102 King St.
1879 to 1882 . . . Dry goods store....................569 King St.
1883 . . . . clothing store........................569 King St.
1889 . . . . clothing store........................505 King St.
1894 . . . . notions store........................505 King St.
1895....................retired
1896....................living upstairs at 333 Green St.

He died on June 19th, 1897, in Charleston, South Carolina, at the age of 60, and was buried there.

Sarah shows up as a widow in 1899 living over 453 King St. The following year she is noted in the census as having had 2 children that are still alive which tallies with what I already mentioned. She also employed a servant. She died at 473 King St. of cerebral apoplexy.

Abraham A Wetherhorn
1844-1887

Spouse	**Mary Ellen Corcoran**
Children	John M Wetherhorn
	Sophie E Wetherhorn p. 44
	Mary R Wetherhorn p. 31
	Rufus M Wetherhorn p. 60
	Elizabeth Wetherhorn

3
Abraham Andrew Wetherhorn

When Abraham Andrew Wetherhorn was born in 1844 in Charleston, South Carolina, his father, Marcus, was 32 and his mother, Tsippora, was 39. He was just 11 years old when his mother died of cholera.

He was still a teen-ager when he became a waggoneer for battery A of the German light artillery based in Charleston. The battery was employed trying to keep federal forces out of Charleston.

St. Mary's church is at 89 Hasell St. The Jewish temple, KKBE, is at 90 Hasell St., across the street and a block or so away. The Wetherhorns were members of the KKBE congregation. There was an Irish Catholic family that apparently attended St. Mary's. Somewhere, Abraham Wetherhorn from one side of the street met Mary Ellen Corcoran from the other. Despite the fact that marriage of Jews outside their own faith was very much frowned upon, even in the relatively liberal KKBE congregation, a romance blossomed. The two were married at St. Mary's on November 9th, 1873. From that point all of Abraham's descendants were Catholic.

The couple lived at 9 John St. in 1874. John St. was not one of the best neighborhoods. In 1875 he was working for A. Jacobs and the couple lived on Mary Street at the corner of Nassau. That year the city directory spelled his name as "Weatherhorne". Later they moved a few houses away to number 15 John. Their son John M. was born on February 22nd, 1876, at that location.

Abraham and Mary's daughter, Sophie Ellen, was born on February 3rd, 1878, in Charleston, South Carolina; she may have been named for his mother, who was known as Sophie in English. In 1877 and 1878 Abraham and his family still lived at 15 John St. He worked as saddler for J. E. Adger & Co. The Adger Company was located at 28 East Bay Street, approximately opposite the Adger Wharf in the port area. That Wharf was one of about 35 that served to make Charleston one of the busier ports on the Eastern seaboard. Most southern ports were locations for shipping cotton. Not Charleston. The lowland area around Charleston was used more for growing rice. It was probably the chief export crop that went from Charleston before the Civil War. In the early post-war period, around 1867, someone discovered large deposits of phosphates in and around Charleston. Phosphates were an important ingredient in agricultural fertilizers. There was a local phosphate boom for over 20 years. Phosphates from Charleston dominated the world market until about 1890. The Ashley Phosphate Company had its office at Adger's wharf. They employed large numbers of men, mostly former slaves, to dig the material up from open pit mines or the river bottoms. One of the streets in North Charleston today is named Ashley Phosphate Road. In 1892 there were over 5000 miners shoveling phosphates. They could earn about $1.75 for a day's work. Once it was dry, the material was loaded into trams for delivery to the wharves. Undoubtedly some of the teams of horses that pulled them used harnesses made by Abraham Wetherhorn.

Daughter Mary Rose was born on April 7th, 1879, in Charleston, South Carolina. By then Abrahams occupation was officially listed as harness maker. In 1881 he was still a harness maker, but employed by A. R. Tomlinson. The Tomlinson commercial address was at 205 Meeting Street. They sold harnesses, among other things. His son Rufus Marion was born on October 24th, 1880, in Charleston, South Carolina. The children grew up at a time when loads of phosphates were constantly being taken to the wharves. In 1889 Charleston shipped about 99% of all the phosphates exported from the US. But by 1910 the market share had dropped to a mere 7% as other countries entered the world market.

Their last child, daughter Elizabeth Irene, was born on July 1st, 1883, in Charleston, South Carolina. She survived less than 2 weeks, dying on July 11th, 1883. Abraham survived her by only a few years. I don't know exactly when he died, but by 1887 his wife showed up as a widow in the city directory. I was told by Matt Vanlandingham that his Uncle John had said

Found its way into several family tree and genealogical sites. I am certain it isn't true. I cannot conceive of a situation where a non-observant Jew who may have even formally converted to Catholicism would be interested in having his body sent to Israel for burial. No one else in his family did so. Such an action would also have been fairly expensive. How could a poor saddle and harness maker afford it? He wasn't even able to leave much for his widow and children when he died.

Having mentioned the children, let's look at what happened to some of them. His widow, who was usually known as Katie, had to look for a way to support herself and her family. She became a housekeeper for Mr. Otto Tiedemann, who owned a large grocery store. Katie and her children lived at 152 Broad Street for several years.

John, the oldest son, was working in the Charleston Bag Factory in 1897. He lived on his own at 25 John St., not far from where he was born. In the following years he moved his residence several times; going to 44 Wentworth St., 3 Wall St., 53 Anson St., and 48 Market St. During that time he worked as a blacksmith or a boilermaker. He never married. He was living with his mother and siblings at 121 Church St. in 1916 when he died of a pulmonary hemorrhage at the age 40 on December 10th, 1916.

Sophie Ellen had married John Patrick Michel in 1897 and they raised their own family, which will be covered in another chapter. In 1910 they had taken in both Katie and Sophie's brother Rufus to their home at 121 Church St. Among the others at that address when the census takers dropped in were 2 teen-age boys listed as Cyrus and Philip Wetherhorn. The boys were aged 15 and 16 at the time. Since Abraham had died over 20 years earlier the actual parents of these 2 is a mystery. I never found any other reference to them in either the Wetherhorn or Michel families.

Rufus went to work as clerk in Tiedemann's store. There was probably a connection to the fact that Katie was Tiedemann's housekeeper. Rufus didn't marry until after his mother died. The two of them lived at 107 Church St. until about 1908 when they moved to 121 Church.

Katie died of heart failure on 31 March 31st, 1927 at the age of 71.

Mary Rose Wetherhorn O'Brien
1879-1950

Spouse	**William R O'Brien**
Children	James R O'Brien
	Mary Jane O'Brien p. 34
	Jeannette O'Brien p. 36
	William J O'Brien Sr. p. 37
	Vincent F O'Brien
	Sophie Ellen O'Brien
	John Joseph O'Brien
	Rita Agnes O'Brien p. 41

Mary Rose, the oldest daughter of Abraham and Katie, was born in Charleston on April 7th, 1879. She married a tall young man who was also of Irish descent, William Richard O'Brien, in 1897. At first, the young couple lived with his parents at 24 Wall Street. Their first son, James Richardson O'Brien, was born on January 5th, 1898. Other children followed about every second year. Mary Jane was born on August 3rd, 1900, Jeanette E. on September 13th, 1902, William Joseph on January 31st, 1905, Vincent Frederick on July 5th, 1907, Sophie Ellen on January 3rd, 1910, John Joseph on June 10th, 1912, and, finally, after a slightly longer break, Rita Agnes on May 24th, 1917. William had found work as a boilermaker at the foundry in Charleston and was so employed in 1910. But the family, including 6 children, was still living with his parents, although by that time they were renting at 53 Anson Street.

The younger O'Brien family later moved to their own rental home at 6 Horlbeck Alley. When the United States entered the First World War William was temporarily unemployed and his hair had already turned grey even though he was only 45 years old.

When their older daughter, Mary Jane, married Ballard Jessee, she and her husband lived with her parents; just as they had lived with his parents when they were first wed.

Son James was underdeveloped, short, and slender. He worked for a while as a newsboy for the Charleston Evening Post. To the best of my knowledge he never married and lived with his mother. I found a death date for someone with the right name and birth date, but it was in Connecticut. I doubt that it refers to the same person.

It appears that Vincent, the younger brother, also never married. He found employment as a call boy at the Port Utility Commission, and later worked as a clerk there. He, too, continued to live at his mother's home.

By 1930 The O'Brien's were still paying $30 a month for rent for their place at 6 Horlbeck Alley. When the census taker came by neither William nor Mary Rose were listed as being employed. Neither were any of the children that were still living at home. That included Sophie, John, Rita, and James, but not Vincent. It also included their 4 year old granddaughter, Anne Theresa Jessee. The 2 older Jessee children were in an orphanage. But that story belongs to another chapter.

In August, 1933, William R. O'Brien started work as a watchman at the West Point Mill in Charleston. He traveled on public transportation. The tram system had gone from horse drawn cars to electric power in 1897, the year Mary Rose and William were married. On September 25th, after being at work for only 1 month, William R. O'Brien was struck by an electric tram on Meeting Street near Cumberland. His skull was fractured. Dr. DeVeaux, the coroner, recorded the incident as an accidental death. His body was turned over to the McAlister undertakers and was buried at the Catholic St. Lawrence Cemetery on September 27th.

The Charleston Probate Court granted Mary Rose fiduciary status for the estate of her late husband on August 9th, 1936. I cannot help but wonder what there was for her to inherit, or why it took nearly 3 years to happen.

Mary Rose continued to keep the home on Horlbeck Alley. James continued to live at home with her. The younger girls married and also initially lived at the family home with their spouses. She died on March 13th, 1950, and was also buried in St. Lawrence Cemetery.

Mary Jane O'Brien Jessee

Spouse	**Lucious E Harley**
Spouse	**Ballard P Jessee**
	Dolores Rose Jessee
	Mary Rita Jessee
	Anne Theresa Jessee

Mary Jane O'Brien was born on August 3rd, 1900 in Charleston.

Her family was living with her grandparents when she married Ballard Preston Jessee on September 22nd, 1919. It might have been a difficult time for them all. Mary Jane was just 19. He served during the First World War as a US Navy Boatswains Mate 2nd class. They started out at her parents' home at 6 Horlbeck. The young couple's first child, daughter Mary Rita, was born was born on May 12th, 1920. I found no data to indicate she was premature, which leaves room for speculation that Mary Jane might have been pregnant when they married. Of course, there's also no proof in the opposite direction.

Ballard did not remain long at the Navy Yard. In 1921 he was working as a bookkeeper for James Richardson. The family now had their own home at 3 Lightwood St. By 1923 he was listed as a salesman and they were living at 52 Laurens St. when daughter number 2, Dolores Rose, was born on March 22nd, 1923. The youngest girl, Anne Theresa, was born on July 24th, 1925. The US Census of 1930 shows that things were not going smoothly. Ballard was listed as an inmate at the National Sanatorium in Johnson City, Tennessee. Mary Jane was renting a room at 42 Vanderhorst in Charleston for $8 a month, and working as a waitress in a hotel. And the girls had become public wards. Mary Rita and Dolores were in the Charleston City Orphan Asylum and little 4 year old Anne Theresa was staying with her grandparents.

What happened in between? I don't really know. In 1927 the entire family had been in Havana, Cuba. They returned to the US aboard the SS CUBA on June 11th. I don't know why they were in Cuba. Possibly there was an employment opportunity. But some- time after that Ballard had some kind of serious problem that led to his admission to Sanatorium in Tennessee. The facility, located at the edge of Johnson City, had been a home for disabled veterans for several years. Following the First World War it became a center for treatment of lung diseases, especially tuberculosis. It is possible Ballard Jessee had contracted the disease. He died there on March 14 th, 1931. The official cause of death was listed as "Acute dilation of Heart – Bilateral Lobar pneumonia". His body was sent to Charleston and interred at the St. Lawrence Catholic Cemetery. Mary Jane likely could not afford to pay for a gravestone. The US Government provided a marker because he was a former serviceman.

Mary Jane married Lucious Edwin Harley on July 25 th, 1932. He was a railway employee and had served in the First World War as a member of the 117th Field Hospital, attached to the 30 th infantry division. It was short marriage. He died on October 1st, 1934 from Peritonitis following his being shot in the abdomen by a pistol on the corner of King and Columbus Streets on September 24th. I don't know if the murderer was apprehended. Once again, Mary Jane turned to the US Government to provide a grave marker.

Mary Jane, herself, died on January 10th,, 1937 of acute ulcerative endocarditis. She had worked in a sewing room for most of the previous year and was only 36 years old when she died. She was buried in St. Lawrence Cemetery 2 days later.

The three girls were now truly orphans. On May 13th 1937 the court appointed Mary Rose O'Brien, their grandmother, as responsible for Mary Rita. The other 2 were assigned to their uncle, John Joseph O'Brien on May 13th, 1938. In fact, they were placed in an orphan home.

Jeanette E O'Brien Huckabee
1902-1975

Spouse — Ralph L Huckabee

Jeannette was born in Charleston on September 13th, 1902. She married Ralph Lawton Huckabee in that same city on June 18th, 1925. He was actually just a bit younger than she. Neither had completed high school. She had dropped out after 1 year, and he did the same after 2 years. After their marriage, he found work as an auto mechanic at the Paul Motor Company. The couple lived with his widowed mother and his siblings, Leroy and Jasper. After his mother found work as a live in matron at the Charleston Orphan Home. Ralph, being the oldest son, took over the family residence. He paid $27.50 a month for rent in 1930. By the following year Ralph had been promoted to shop foreman. He was also elected as Junior Warden of Friendship Lodge number 9. His brothers soon married and moved into their own new homes and Ralph and Jeannette lived at 64 King Street. He also began working as a salesman for Paul Motor Company. The 1931 City Directory shows them with telephone number 5213.The Huckabees seem to have been a typical lower middle class (or possibly upper lower class) couple. They did manage to survive the Great Depression. Neither had much education, and probably never aspired to much more than to live happily with each other.

It appears that the couple wasn't able to maintain a home on their own. In 1940 Ralph and Jeannette were back at 4 Horlbeck, living with her mother and some of her siblings. I found no record of their ever having children. He died on August 2nd, 1967 and she on July 14th, 1975. They are buried side by side in the Catholic community's St. Lawrence Cemetery.

William J O'Brien
1905-1957

Spouse   Clara F George

Children   Dorothy C O'Brien

                    William J O'Brien Jr

On January 31st, 1905 William J O'Brien was born in Charleston, SC. He grew up with his siblings in Charleston. At age 25 he separated from the family and married Clara F. George. She was 2 years younger than he. The marriage took place on October 19th, 1928.

The couple's first child, daughter Dorothy Claire, was born on January 10th, 1931, 3 weeks before her father's 26th birthday. A second child, this time a boy, named William Joseph Jr., was born on February 4 th, 1932.

William was working as a switchman for Charleston D D & M in 1930 and Clara was employed as a clerk at the oil refinery. They rented a home at 125 Meeting Street for $20 a month. To help out economically they took in a roomer. He was Charles Angelo, a Greek immigrant, who opened a fruit stand in town.

By 1934 William was working as a fireman at Engine Company 2 located at the corner of Meeting Street and Wentworth. The Charleston Fire Department had almost 100 firefighters enrolled. The O'Briens were living at 89b Logan Street, just off of Queen Street. They needed a larger home for the children. By 1940 they had moved to 107 Alexander Street where the rent was $30 a month. Clara's 20 year old sister, Margaret George, lived with them. By this time his annual salary was $1400. As a fireman, and being always on call, he often put in a work week of up to 76 hours.

Their lives beyond 1940 are outside the scope of this book, but I do want to mention that William died of lung cancer on

October 31st, 1957. They were living at 830 Rutledge at that time, and he was the captain of the same fire engine company he had originally joined. He was buried in the St. Andrews Parish Cemetery, Live Oak Memorial Garden, on November 2nd, 1957.

Clara was buried in the same place after her death in June 1986.

John Joseph O'Brien
1912-1978

Spouse	**Helen Parker**
Children	Patricia Anne O'Brien

John Joseph O'Brien was the seventh child of Mary Rose Wetherhorn and William O'Brien. He was born in Charleston on June 10th, 1912.

When the US census taker came to his parents' home on January 5th, 1920 John was living with his parents, and all his siblings, at 6 Horlbeck Alley. It even included his older sister's husband, Ballard Jessee. The home was rented. The city of Charleston had become an incorporated entity in 1899, just before the previous census.

Most of his family was at the same home when the next census took place on April 4 th, 1930. It was still a rented home and his father paid $30 a month for it. But by then Sophie, James and Rita were the only siblings still at home. The census taker did record Mary Ballard's youngest daughter at her grandparents' home. Her father had been placed in an institution, and her older siblings were in an orphanage. The house was on the North side of the street, next to Ashley Auto Sales Corporation. All the homes on one side of the business were occupied by white families, while those on the other side were all colored families.

John found work at the paper mill where he was employed as a Jordan operator. Yes, that's correct. What is a Jordan operator? I had no idea when I first read the job description. I had heard of the Jordan River, and eaten Jordan almonds. But what was a Jordan operator? Well, I looked around and discovered that a Jordan was a refiner that allowed a measure of control over the mixture of pulp that was about to become paper. The Jordan operator could make variations that determined the quality of the paper. It allowed John to leave his childhood home for place of his own. He rented a house at 778 Rutledge. That was where he brought his bride when he married Helen Parker on the First of June, 1936.

The new home was much further to the North, but not quite as far in that direction as the cemeteries, Both KKBE and St. Lawrence were located slightly more to the north and east.

The Charleston Navy Yard became a major source of new work for people in the area when the Government decided in 1933 that the yard would be a site for construction of new warships. A dry dock was constructed and new roads were paved under WPA projects, many of which started in 1935.

Another investment project took the form of construction of new school buildings. Between 1916 and 1929 Charleston built 19 new schools for whites and 12 more for blacks. Segregation was still the rule in those days. One of the "white" schools was the Chicora High school. It was constructed primarily for the Chicora Indian community that was located in and near Charleston. The Chicora were one of about 29 native Indian tribes that originally lived in South Carolina. They only numbered a few hundred at that time. The Chicora had always been an agricultural tribe, engaged in raising beans, tobacco, and domesticated animals that included chickens and deer. In the 21st century whatever remained of the Chicora seems to have been assimilated into the Gullah-Geechee, a group primarily descended from former West African slaves that live along the Carolina coast.

On May 13th, 1938 John Joseph O'Brien became a fiduciary for his nieces Dolores Rose Jessee and Anne Theresa Jessee. The girl's mother had died. The 2 sisters were assigned to their uncle. In fact, they had already been placed in an orphan home.

Helen Parker was born on May 30th, 1914 in a rural area near Augusta, Georgia. She presented John with a daughter, Patricia Anne, in 1939. The girl attended Bishop England High School. As far as I know, she never married.

John died at age 66 on June 14th, 1978, He was buried in North Augusta, Aiken County, South Carolina.

On August 18th, 1978, probate Case 078-0062 was heard in Charleston. Helen P. O'Brien was made fiduciary. She died on March 31st, 1989 and was buried near her husband.

Rita Agnes Obrien Rourke
1917-2011

Spouse	**StClair Harley Rourke**
Children	William Richard Rourke
	Sandra StClair Rourk
	Gail Rourk

The youngest of the O'Brien children, Rita Agnes, was born on May 24 th, 1917. When she was 2 years old John Patrick Grace was elected to a second term as mayor of Charleston. He had previously served in that post from 1911 to 1915. Grace had Irish Catholic family roots and was outspokenly anti British. This may have been why he was not re-elected in 1916. But he was also a solid progressive and dedicated public servant. He also had no qualms about bribery and fraud. As mayor, he banned cows and livestock from the city streets as a public health measure. He also set about paving those streets with asphalt. The ones around the harbor were cobblestoned and others were brick. But many were just dirt. When he left the office of mayor, and following an unsuccessful venture into Florida land development, he joined the Cooper River Bridge Company. His political connections probably helped secure some funding for the project. The original cost estimate was $3,000,000. The company hired the New York firm of Waddell and Hardesty to design the structure. It was actually made of two parts. The first section went up from the Charleston side over Town Creek to Drum Island. The second part went from Drum Island over the Cooper River to Mount Pleasant. The entire structure was a connected cantilever bridge that was 2.71 miles long and was even higher than the famous Brooklyn Bridge. When it was completed, at a cost of $6 million, it was the largest structure of its kind in the world. The section spanning Town Creek was aimed more to the East. The bridge then curved over Drum Island and went more to the North as it crossed the Cooper River. The roadway had 2 lanes, one in each direction, and they were only 10 feet wide with no shoulders. The combination of going up and down and up and down while changing directions made the crossing remind some people of a roller coaster. The toll for crossing was 50 cents for an automobile. That was a serious sum in those days.

When the bridge Opened, in August 1929, the former ferry boat service from Mount Pleasant was out of business. The Cooper River Bridge would later be named the John P. Grace Memorial Bridge. A second bridge was later built alongside the first to handle increased traffic flow. Maintenance, however, was not a strong point for the South Carolina Highway Department. The bridges lacked many safety features that became standard over the years. Ultimately, the bridges were replaced by a new structure and the old ones were dismantled.

Rita grew up as part of a typical Catholic family in Charleston. She went to Bishop England High School. That was the Catholic school of choice for many families in the city. She met St. Clair Harley Rourk, who was year older than she. They were married in Charleston on February 25 th, 1937. Their first child, William Richard Rourk, was born on August 6th, 1937. The extended family lived at 4 Horlbeck. That included her widowed mother, her brother James, and her sister Jeannette with Jeannette's husband Ralph Huckabee. In 1940 Ralph was a car salesman and St. Clair worked as the assistant manager of a filling station. His monthly salary of $780 covered the $25 a month rent and left enough to spare for other essentials as well as providing for their growing family. .

Although much of her adult life is outside the date limitations of this book, there are some items I want to mention, First, Rita worked for the local Piggly-Wiggly grocery store for about 25 years. She was also a volunteer with the Charleston County Voter Registration Board.

It was scary world she originally came into. On April 6 th, 1917, two days after the U.S. Senate voted 82 to 6 to declare war against Germany, the U.S. House of Representatives endorsed the decision by a vote of 373 to 50. The United States was now an official belligerent in the Great War. It would later become better known as the First World War. The week before Rita was born the Selective Service Act of 1916 went into effect. That law allowed the US Government to raise a large army by conscription. There had been conscription during the US Civil War, and it was not popular then. That older law also allowed a draftee to provide a substitute for his own service. This was usually done by paying someone a bounty to go in his place. The 1917 law omitted that feature. Ultimately, about 2.8 million men were inducted into the army under the provisions of the law. Some 2 million other Americans volunteered for service. Volunteering allowed an individual a little choice in which branch of the service he would serve. The only one of Rita's siblings that had to register was her older brother, James. He was exempted as being underdeveloped.

She had 3 children. And at the time of her death on September 26 [th], 2011 there were 6 grandchildren and 6 great-grandchildren.

Her husband, St. Clair Harley Rourk, preceded her in death. He passed away in Mount Pleasant on October 3rd, 1986.

They are both buried in Mount Pleasant Memorial Gardens.

Sophie Ellen Wetherhorn Michel
1878-1949

Spouse	**John Patrick Michel**
Children	Mary Ellen Michel
	Charles James Michel p. 48
	Rosalie J Michel p. 50
	Sophie Ellen Michel p. 52
	John P Michel Jr p. 54
	Rufus L Michel p. 56
	Agnes Cecile Michel p. 59
	Joseph L Michel
	Celestine Mary Michel
	Daniel James Michel

In Chapter 3 I noted that Sophie was born in 1878 when her parents were living at 15 John Street in Charleston.

She married John Patrick Michel when she was only 19. He came from a French-Canadian Catholic family, while she was Irish Catholic on her mother's side and German Jewish from her father. Their first residence was at 19 John Street, where her parents lived. He worked as a clerk for H. J. O'Neill.

In 1901 The Federal Government made an important decision. A new Navy Yard was to be opened at Charleston. It replaced older facilities at Port Royal that had been in use since the Civil War. The new base was located up the Cooper River North West of the city. It would become a major employer for Charleston residents. Port Royal was formally closed in 1903.

By 1903 the Michel family was residing at 107 Church Street and John Patrick was a blacksmith at W. F. Bresnihan's stone and marble works. The yard was located at 134 Meeting Street and his employer lived a short distance away from them at 132 Church

As their family grew Sophie and John were forced to move back in to the old family home at 121 Church Street. In 1910 the house was officially rented by Sophie's mother and they shared the home with her brothers John and Rufus. The biggest family was their own, as they already had 5 children by then. Husband John tried to earn a living from his own blacksmith shop. Sophie also worked as a stenographer while caring for their offspring. On August 19th, 1915 they were visited by a tragedy when their newborn son, Joseph L. died only 2 months after his birth.

By 1920 the house was officially rented by John. He was then working as a general contractor. Rufus was still living with them at the same address. They now had 9 children. They took in a boarder, the museum custodian, to help defray the costs.

The 1923 city directory shows they had a telephone, number 3619. Everyone in the family shared the number. By then the 2 older girls, Mary Ellen and Rosalie were working as stenographers, and Charles, who dropped out of school after the 7th grade, had found employment with Southern Bell Telephone and Telegraph.

Mary Ellen, the oldest girl, contracted Tuberculosis. It spread into her intestines. She underwent an operation on May 2nd, 1928 in an attempt to solve her health problems, but it was not a success. She died on July 5th and was buried 2 days later in the St. Lawrence Catholic Cemetery.

The 1930 census shows them still at the same address. The rent then was $20/month. John and his son Charles were working as tile layers in construction. By 1934 he had created his own marble and tile laying business, John P. Michel and Sons. Both Charles and John P. Jr. were working with him.

This is a good place to mention the 2 youngest children, Celestine Mary Michel and Daniel James Michel. Neither of them ever married and therefore don't have separate pages in this story. Celestine was always known in the family as "Teenie". She was born on February 14th, 1917. Her brother Daniel was born on June 16th, 1919. Both completed high school and both worked as office clerks or stenographers during the period of this history. The 1940 census even says they were receiving the same pay for their 40 hour work weeks, but in different offices. Both eventually moved to Mount Pleasant. Teenie died there On October 15th, 1996 and her brother Daniel died there on May 5th, 2003.

The Parents, John Patrick and Sophie Ellen Michel had preceded them. John passed away on September 21st, 1948. Sophie Ellen died on August 6th, 1949. Both had remained at 121 Church Street until their deaths.

The following photograph of the family was taken on the occasion of the 50th anniversary of Sophie Ellen and John Patrick. The list of the people that follows the picture is exactly what accompanied the photo when it was sent to me. I believe it originally came from John Torlay. Several of the younger children were born after the 1940 cut-off date for this book.

First Row:

Anthony Rufus Michel, Jr., William Thomas Michel, John Michel, Jr. (Johnsie – son of John and Mary Michel), little girl holding stuffed animal unknown, maybe Mary Ellen Marcil, Chrissy Michel Murphy (daughter of John & Mary), Ruth Michel Van Landingham, 90% sure Mary Ann Michel (not sure of her spelling – daughter of John & Mary), Kay Michel Polsgrove, maybe Janice Michel (daughter of John & Mary), John Michel.

Second Row:

Daniel Michel, Mary Blanchard (daughter of John & Rosalie Blanchard), Rosalie Michel Blanchard, the baby she is holding is possibly Gene Blanchard (I'm guessing boy Gene instead of girl Jean), girl in front of baby is Agnes Blanchard (daughter of John & Rosalie), next to her is Joseph Lawrence Michel, boy behind Larry is John Blanchard, Jr. (son of John & Rosalie), next to Larry is Celestine Michel, boy behind Celestine is John Torlay, Jr. (son of John & Sophie), then Grandmother & Grandfather (Ellen Sophie Wetherhorn & John Patrick Michel), next to Grandfather is Rufus Marion Wetherhorn (Bubba Rufus, Grandmother's brother), his wife Mary Barr Wetherhorn, Mary Collins Michel who married John Michel.

Third Row:

John Blanchard, Jean Marcil, baby unknown, Agnes Michel Marcil, Sophie Michel Torlay, John Torlay, Father James May, Helen Torlay Gay (daughter of John & Sophie), Frances Schrott Michel, Rufus Lawrence Michel, Robert Douglas Michel.

Charles James Michel 1902-1961	
Spouse	**Dovie West Finch**
Spouse	**Mollie Collins**
Children	Mary Anne Michel
	Christine Michel
	Janice R Michel

Charles was introduced in the chapter about his parents. He followed in his father's path after high school and joined him in the family business, along with his brother John Patrick Jr.

About 1926 Charles married Mollie Collins. She was original from Arkansas and trained as a hairdresser. She would use that experience to later open her own salon in Charleston name "A La-Mode Beauty Shoppe". Mollie was about a year younger than her husband.

The couple initially lived at the Michel family home at 121 Church St. Later, they moved to 159 Calhoun Street which was where they were still living in 1940 when this history comes to an official end. By then they had 2 daughters, Mary Anne, known in the family as Maemae, and Christine. These two were born at the two ends of the year 1936. It must have been hard to handle two infants so close together in age.

They had another little girl in 1945. Janice.

I found the family living at 104 Queen Street in 1940 when they were both listed by the census taker as being employed in private retail sales. Their neighbors at 104 Queen were Charles' sister, Sophie Ellen and her husband John T. Torlay.

Charles and Mollie divorced in 1940. He later remarried, in 1945. But that, of course, is also outside the scope of this family history.

Working as a tile setter in the family construction firm was not a particularly high prestige job. It also wasn't a particularly high paying job. But it did provide steady employment. It probably also had some hazards associated with it. When Charles registered for the draft in 1942 they noted he had scars on his left arm and his hair was already grey. He was registered as being 5′ 7 ½ "tall.

He was not called up for military service.

Charles died of natural causes on October 3rd, 1951 in Roper Hospital at 234 Hugin St. in Charleston. He was buried in the Catholic St. Lawrence Cemetery.

Rosalie J Michel Blanchard
1904-1985

Spouse	**John E Blanchard**
Children	Mary R Blanchard
	John E Blanchard Jr
	Agnes C Blanchard
	Sophie E Blanchard
	Eugene S Blanchard

Rosalie J. Blanchard was born May 4th, 1904. After completing High School she found employment as an office stenographer for Charles S. Glover's insurance located at 42 Broad Street.

Meanwhile, John Edward Blanchard was working as a clerk at the A. C. L. freight depot which extended along the length of the port. John was living with his widowed mother and 2 sisters at 30-A Bull Street. The two individuals met and soon married. The marriage took place in Charleston on June 12th, 1931.

By 1940 they had 3 children; Mary R., age 6, John Edward Jr., age 5, and little Agnes Comer, age 2. These 3 would later be joined by 2 more. The family moved to Sullivan's Island where Edward and Rosalie remained until their deaths.

This seems to be a good place for a small aside about Sullivan's Island. This town as of 2010 is one of the most affluent in the state of South Carolina. The population is relatively small, but each home is located on a plot of one and a half acres. That was a requirement from when the town was founded. With that fact in mind,

one would not have suspected that the island, where old Fort
Moultrie was situated, was once, before the civil war, the major
port of entry for slaves arriving from Africa. There was a
quarantine station located on Sullivan's Island and all arriving
slaves spent a 10 day period there before being moved on to the
Charleston Slave Market. According to some estimates, about
400,000 slaves were imported into the South and about 40% of
them passed through Charleston. That would make Sullivan's
Island the largest entry point for slaves in the entire South.
Something like Ellis Island was for European immigrants
coming to the United States.

Edward and Rosalie Blanchard are buried in Mount Pleasant
Memorial Gardens.

Sophie Ellen Michel Torlay
1906-1992

Spouse   John Thomas Torlay

Children   Agnes Ann Torlay

                    Sophie Helen Torlay

                    John T Torlay Jr

                    Robert A Torlay

                    Annette Marie Torlay

Sophie Ellen, named for her mother, was born in Charleston on July 15th, 1906. The picture was cropped from a family photo of her parents golden wedding anniversary.

She was the 4th of 11 siblings. She married John Thomas Torlay in Charleston on August 27th, 1931. He was a plumber and worked in the family business at 32 Beaufain St.

The Torlay family grew rapidly. Daughter Agnes Ann was born on February 16th, 1932. Daughter Sophie Helen followed on November 29th, 1932. Son John Thomas Junior was born on June 29th, 1934. The lives of these three are outside the time frame of the book and therefore there will be no further mention of them. What I will mention is that on April 5th, 1933, between the births of the Torlay children, the United States officially left the Gold Standard as a guarantee for American currency. In doing so, the US followed in the steps of Great Britain who had done the same thing in 1931. The step was one of many taken to try to bring the US out of the Great Depression that had started with the collapse of the US Stock Market on

October 29th, 1929. The Torlays, and others mentioned in this history, were never speculators in finance. They did not "play" the stock market. But they, and all Americans, had their lives profoundly affected by it.

Robert Anthony Torlay was born on March 27th 1937. He contracted acute encephalitis and died on September 11th, 1939 when he was only 2 years and 5 months old.

The last child, Annette Marie, was born on November 24th. 1941. She suffered from Microcephalus from birth. She died on September 17th,. 1942, after a short life of only 9 months. At that time the family was living at 102 Queen Street. They were members of the congregation at Christ Our King Catholic Church.

At a later date the family moved to Mount Pleasant. John died there in February 1983 and Sophie Ellen followed on October 22nd, 1992.

John Patrick Michel jr
1909-1987

Spouse   **Mary Viola Collins**

Children   Christine Marie Michel

                Mary Ann Michel

                John P Michel III

John Patrick Michel Jr. was born in Charleston on April 30 [th], 1909

He married Mary Viola Collins September 7th, 1934 in Charleston.

She was born in Charleston on November 10th, 1911.

John was 5' 6" tall and weighed 175 pounds when he was registered for the draft in 1942. He had black hair and brown eyes.

Crossing the Atlantic in the air was a big thing when he was younger. The US Navy made the trip in 1919 with the flight of the NC-4. So did the British team of Alcock and Brown, but in the opposite direction. They were followed a few weeks later by the British airship R-34. But the biggest headlines were reserved for Charles Lindbergh who made the first solo flight in 1927. Newspapers wrote about it and the newsreels in the film theaters carried pictures of him landing.

John Torlay originally worked with his father as a tile setter but by 1940 he had moved on to being a salesman for Atlantic Paint Co. and earned about $1500 a year.

The Atlantic Paint Company was located at 207 Meeting Street. The front of the store had a prominent display saying "Dutch Boy Paints". I found an interesting note about them that actually is outside the time frame. In 1944 a number of companies, including Atlantic Paint, formed the Charleston Development Board with the objective of "finding peacetime solutions for war- time industries". Their records are on file with the South Carolina Historical Society. This, of course, has nothing to do with the Michel family.

Their daughter Mary Ann was born in 1935. A second daughter, Christine, whom everyone called Chrissie, followed a year later, and a son, John Patrick III, nicknamed Johnsie, followed in 1941.

In 1940 they lived at 102 Queen Street in a home valued at $4000.

John Patrick Jr. died on June 25th, 1987 and was buried in Holy Cross Cemetery on James Island,

Viola later remarried. She died on October 3rd. 2004. She was buried alongside John Patrick Jr.

Anthony Rufus (Rufus Lawrence) Michel
1911-1984

Spouse   Frances A Schrott

Children   Joseph   L   Michel

                       Anthony   R   Michel

                       Mary   Ruth   Michel

                       William Thomas Michel

                       Kathryn   T   Michel

                       Robert D Michel

                       John T Michel

                       Elizabeth Ann Michel

Anthony Rufus Michel was born in Charleston on July 15th, 1911. He was born as Anthony Rufus Michel, and later in life changed his name legally to Rufus Lawrence. But most of his life he was known as Mike. He may have received the nickname to avoid confusion with his uncle, Rufus Wetherhorn, who lived in the same house with the Michel family for several years.

Mike attended Charleston's Catholic Bishop England High School where he played basketball for the school team, despite the fact that he was just 5′ 8 ½″ tall. In 1931 the team participated in the All Catholic High School tournament at Loyola University in Chicago. The team didn't win the tournament, but Mike was awarded the Bishop England Cup for having committed the fewest fouls during the competition. He went on to spend the difficult early years of the Great Depression as a university student. He also married Frances Anita Schrott in Washington, DC on May 2nd, 1936.

After Mike completed his degree he found work in various jobs around the country. It wasn't easy. The entire US was still in the midst of the Great Depression. GDP had immediately dropped by 15%. International trade fell by half. Unemployment went from 5% to 23%, an increase of 607%. American Industrial production between 1929 and 1932.had dropped by 46 per cent. In 1930 many US banks began to fail. This wiped out peoples savings completely. There was no Federal Deposit Insurance Corporation yet. That would only come when Roosevelt had it created in an attempt to restore confidence in the banking system. Oh yes, and to make matters worse, a series of dust storms hit the central states and drove hundreds of farm families away from their homes.

The trail of the Michel family's temporary homes can be traced by looking at the birthplaces of their older children. For example; their first child, Joseph Lawrence, known as Larry, was born in St. Paul, Minnesota. Child number two, Anthony Rufus Junior, nicknamed Rukie, was born in Lafayette, Indiana on June 23rd, 1938. Their third child, daughter Mary Ruth, was born in Columbus Ohio on December 10th, 1939. At that time Mike was working as a receiver in a warehouse in that city. In 1940 things changed a bit. Mike got a government job as an auditor for the state of South Carolina. The family moved to Columbia where they lived at 1223 Butler Street. Mike paid $37 a month rent out of his $2300 annual salary for that home.

By the end of 1940 Mike had a new government job. He went to work for the Federal Government in the new General Accountability Office (GAO). The Budget and Accounting Act of 1921 formed GAO to investigate all matters related to the use of public funds. Mike was assigned to the California office located at 2286 Fulton Street in Berkeley, California. Their third son, William Thomas, known as Tommy, was born in Oakland on December 7th, 1940.

Mike and Frances had 4 more children later. He died in Arlington, VA, on November 19th, 1984, and was buried in the National Cemetery there. Frances survived until December 29th, 2003 and was buried in the same location.

Agnes Cecile Michel Marcil
1913-2001

Spouse   **Joseph St J Marcil**

Children   Mary Ellen Marcil

Jeanne Marie Marcil

Agnes Ann Marcil

Joseph St J Marcil Jr

Agnes Cecile Michel was born in Charleston on September 13th, 1913. She finished high school and worked as a stenographer before marrying Joseph St. Jean Marcil on May 30th, 1939. He was almost a year younger than she.

Most of their lives are outside the scope of dates for this family history; I will note that they raised 4 children; 3 girls and a boy. Joe died on Wednesday, May 13th, 1992 in Mount Pleasant and was buried in Mount Pleasant Memorial Gardens after a short service at Christ Our King Catholic Church. Agnes died on July 2nd, 2001, also in Mount Pleasant.

Rufus Marion Wetherhorn
1880-1967

Spouse   **Mary Bertha Barr**

Children   Nancy B Wetherhorn

Rufus Marion Wetherhorn was born in Charleston on October 24th, 1880. His father died when he was only 7 years old. His mother had to struggle to survive as the family was never financially well off. Part of that story is covered in the chapter on his parents,

Rufus continued to live with his mother until her death. He was employed by I. M. Pearlstine as a sales- man for a while. Soon after that he took a wife. Mary Bertha Barr was born on October 4th, 1889. They never had children of their own. In 1934 they were living at 1199 King Street and Rufus had his own business, Wetherhorn's Luncheonette, at 153 Calhoun. It was not a success.

In 1940 the US Census records him as having been unemployed for 78 weeks. That same year shows Nancy Buck, then reported as their niece, living with them. I never found formal adoption records, but

Abraham A Wetherhorn 1844-1887

when Nancy married in 1960 she listed her name as Nancy Buck Wetherhorn.

Rufus died in Charleston on March 7th, 1967 and Mary died there on May 13th, 1977. They are buried, side by side, in Bethany Cemetery.

Solomon Wetherhorn
1840-1917

Spouse   **Lena Brandt**

Children   Julius Wetherhorn   p. 67

              Sophie Wetherhorn   p. 71

              Marcus Wetherhahn

              Mitchell Wetherhahn

              Arthur Wetherhorn   p. 73

              Philip Wetherhahn

              Pauline Wetherhorn

              Blume Wetherhorn

              Sarah Wetherhorn   p. 82

              Louis L. Wetherhorn   p. 86

              Adolph Wetherhorn   p. 88

              Bertha Wetherhorn   p. 90

4
Solomon Wetherhorn

Solomon Wetherhorn was born in Hannover, Niedersachsen, Germany on December 7th 1840. He was just a tiny infant when the family left Europe to move to America.

The family probably spoke German or Yiddish at home.

His family life was severely interrupted when he was just 14. His mother died from cholera. When his father remarried in 1857 it appears that Solomon, and his brothers, all decided to move out. The decision may have been aided by the growing tensions between the Northern and Southern states.

All the Wetherhorn boys appear to have tried to join the military for the coming war. Solomon had an interesting career with the Confederate Army. He first joined the 25th South Carolina Infantry regiment, also known as the Eutaw Regiment.

He was a private in Company E of that unit. The 25th was stationed near Charleston for most of the early part of the war. During that time Solomon actually served with his brothers in Captain Wagener's Battery of the German Light Artillery. He appears on he appears on their muster rolls as a temporary substitute for H. Eckmann. Solomon was admitted to the Episcopal Church Hospital in May 1864 complaining of various palpitations but was released in June 1864 and apparently traveled north to rejoin his regiment. The 25th South Carolina had been moved north to help defend Richmond as part of a South Carolina brigade under General Hagood. The entire brigade was thrown in to battle at Weldon Railroad Station on August 21st, 1864 in an attempt to recapture the last remaining railroad link for bringing supplies to Robert E. Lee's army at Richmond. The attack failed and the 25th South Carolina regiment had 2 men killed, 29 wounded, and 70 missing. Solomon Wetherhorn was one of the missing. He had actually been shot in the stomach and was captured by Union forces. This is a list of prisoners from Federal records. Sol appears 3 lines above the tear on the bottom left side of the document.

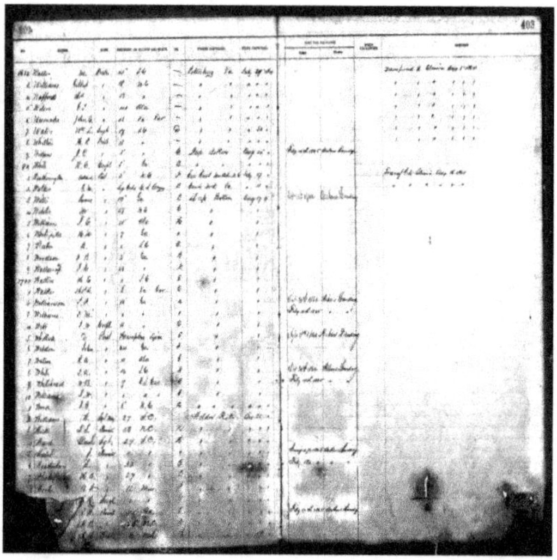

Solomon was traded in a prisoner ex- change at Aikens Landing on February 18th, 1865. Solomon did not return to Charleston. It is possible that his father thought he had been killed because he named his next son by his second wife Solomon. It is common for Jews to name a newborn in honor of a relative that has died previously.

When the War ended Charleston was just the burnt out shell of what had been a thriving city. Federal aid was definitely not forthcoming. The Reconstruction congress was out to punish South Carolina for having had a leading role in secession. Charleston was, after all, the place where the first shots were fired. Solomon decided to start a new life in Augusta, Georgia. In 1870 he shows up in the census living with the Kaufman family there. Julius Kaufman ran a clothing store, and Solomon was employed as clerk in the store.

Sol soon met Lena Brandt and the two were married on March 15 th 1871 by Rabbi Aaron Blum. Reverend Blum was head of Augusta's Reform Congregation Children of Israel from 1869 to 1872.

The couple initially settled in Waynesboro, Georgia. They had twelve children in the next 22 years. Seven of them have their own chapters. Pauline, who was born in January 1884 and died on March 17th, 1905 of acute pneumonia while visiting in Augusta, doesn't have her own chapter because she never married. There are 4 others who died as infants; Marcus, born in 1885 and died on September 5 th, 1876,

Mitchell, born 1877 and died April 15th, 1878, Philip, born 1881 and died April 21st, 1885, and Blume, born 1885 and died August 15th, 1886. All were buried in Magnolia Cemetery in Augusta, Georgia. All, including their parents, spelled their last name as Wetherhahn in cemetery records.

Sol was involved in a lot of things during his life. An 1895 item in *The Atlanta Constitution* (June 24 p 4) credits him with producing some extraordinary farm crops. Of particular note was a twin squash on a single stem. The 8 May 1902 edition (p 6) reports he was elected as the coroner in Waynesboro. I am unaware of his having any kind of medical training, but that might not have been a consideration then, He was still at that job in May 1909 when there is a report of him presiding over an inquest as coroner. One family legend says that there were 2 civil war cannon placed at the entrance to the Waynesboro Burke County Courthouse, and that Sol was the person responsible for acquiring them.

In the official documents sphere the 1880 Federal Census shows the family, Sol, Lena, and 4 children, living Waynesboro in a rented house. Lena's father, Helman, and brother, Louis, were living with them at that time. By 1900 they were renting a house at 8 Liberty Street. Six of the children were still with them, but Lena's father and brother were no longer there. That report says Sol worked as a merchant and his son, Arthur, worked as a salesman in Solomon's Dry Goods.

Solomon encountered some problems with the way his name was recorded. At various times he was Sol, Solomon, and even John Solomon. The family name was spelled Wetterhahn. Wetherhahn, Wetherhorn, Weatherhorn, and even Witterhorn. Lena passed away on September 17, 1908, in Augusta, Georgia, at the age of 57. They had been married 37 years.

Augusta Georgia is located about half way between Charleston and Atlanta. Waynesboro is located a short distance south of Augusta. With the in one of six apartments in a building at 315 Oglethorpe children grown and Lena gone, Waynesboro was apparently not a place where Sol wished to remain. In 1914 He was living in Savannah with his son Louis. They had a telephone (number 1698-J) so he might have been in touch with his sister-in-law

Bertha. This is not his daughter Bertha. She has her own chapter. This Bertha was the widow of Sol's younger brother, Henry Wetherhorn. She resided at 307 36th St. in Savannah. Other family members in Savannah at the time included Adolph and Viola, and his daughter Sophie and her husband Peter S. Deck. The apartment on Oglethorpe was actually rented by Deck. Louis soon moved out to a place of his own. When Solomon died at age 76 on August 15th, 1917 he left no will. Peter Deck applied to the probate court to handle the estate. There is a hand written entry in an old family prayer book that says Solomon died on Wednesday, August 15th, 1917 at 10:30 AM.

Sol and Lena are buried in Magnolia Cemetery in Augusta Georgia.

Julius   Wetherhorn
1871-1953

Spouse	**Lillie McNair**
Children	? Wetherhorn
	Infant girl Wetherhorn
	Lillian B Wetherhorn p. 69
	Lena Mae Wetherhorn p. 70
	Jane E Wetherhorn p. 70

Julius Wetherhorn was born in Waynesboro, Burke County, Georgia, on the last day of August, 1871. In October of that year the worst forest fire disaster in US history occurred in the Northeast corner of Wisconsin. The fire is usually called the Peshtigo Fire, after a small lumber town that was almost totally wiped out by it. It is also the name of the river that ran through the town. The fire destroyed over 1,200,000 acres of timberland and killed about 1500 people. By way of contrast, the great Chicago Fire that took place on the same day destroyed 2,350 acres of the city and killed only 300 people. Everybody knows about the Chicago Fire. Most have never heard of the Peshtigo Fire.

When Julius was 24, on October 20th, 1895, he married Lillie -

Catherine McNair. The couple had been married 5 years when the first of their 5 daughters was born. Julius worked as sales clerk in a department store. The family lived in a rented home on Jones Street in Augusta Georgia. This would be the pattern for their lives for the next several years. There is a gravestone in the Augusta

Magnolia Cemetery which was placed to mark the side by side resting places of two unnamed infant girls. The records say they were the daughters of Mr. and Mrs. J. Wetherhorn. In the absence of any other data, no dates are indicated; I suspect these may have been children of Julius and Lillie. It also helps explain the gap between the birth of their first child in 1900 and the birth dates of the other 2 girls in 1911 and 1914.

Julius continued to work as a salesman, but changed his place of employment from time to time. Similarly, their rented home was not always at the same address. They rented about 5 different places over the years, all located near the intersection of Fifth and Ellis. By 1940 there were only two daughters living at home. Julius was temporarily employed as a night watchman at a wholesale warehouse, and Jane, the only girl still at home, was working wrapping candies.

Lillie died on August 15th, 1946. Julius died on February 17th, 1952. They are both buried in the Westview Cemetery in Augusta.

Lillian B Wetherhorn
1900-1976

Spouse	**Henry Harvard**
Children	Henry J Harvard Sr.
	Dorothy C Harvard
	William F Harvard
	Jack McNair Harvard

Julius and Lillie had three daughters, all of whom lived beyond the cutoff year for this history of 1940. The oldest was Lillian B. born December 21st, 1900 in Augusta. It wasn't until 1910 that her sister Jane was born. Lena Mae, most often known as Mae or May, followed on September 22nd, 1911.

It appears that the girls all went to Tubman High School for Girls at 1740 Walton Way in Augusta, GA. The school was not named in honor of Harriet Tubman of civil rights fame. It was named for the founder, Emily Harvie Thomas Tubman, a well-known philanthropist and supporter of girls' education in her day. It was the only public high school for girls in the area at the time. This picture of Jane, at the bottom of p. 70 below, comes from the 1930 Tubman School yearbook. She was about 16 at the time.

Her sister Lena Mae is listed with the sophomore class in the 1927 school yearbook.

Jane is listed as Jane E. Weatherhorn and was often called Jennie. Her sister Lena Mae was called Mae or May most of the time. The family name shows up as Weatherhorn or Wetherhorn in different places.

Lillian, the oldest daughter, married when she was 18 or 19. Her husband, Henry Fletcher Harvard, was about 4 years older. They originally lived with her family at 301 Stolleck Avenue. Henry worked as a dry goods salesman for C. H. Schnieder and Son. His father in law was also a salesman at a dry goods store. Their first son was born on August 19th, 1919. He was named Henry Julian, possibly in honor of both his father and grandfather. The Harvards soon moved to their own rented home at 1331 Ellis. Daughter Dorothy Cornelia was born on November 3rd, 1921. A second son, William Fletcher, followed on May 31 st, 1925. Their last child, Jack McNair Fletcher was born on August 7th, 1928.

Henry Julian Fletcher completed 3 years of high school. His education was probably cut short by the Depression. He was working as a serviceman for Sears Roebuck and Co. when he registered for the selective service. The form noted he was 6'1" tall, but weighed only 133#. He married Wilma D. Wilkerson, and further events of their lives are beyond the scope of this history.

Lena Mae Wetherhorn
1911-1976

Spouse	**Irving Rosen**
Children	Lois Rosen

Returning to Lena Mae Wetherhorn I found she appears to have married a carpenter from South Carolina named James Allen Youmans. He died of a heart attack and she later married Irving Rosen, a freelance photographer. They lived in Hawaii.

It is actually outside the scope of this history, but Mae had an active and interesting life. She raised Persian and Siamese cats and hosted a radio show on station KNDI in Hawaii called "Cat Chat". Mae also painted cats on velvet, signing her work as "Mayo". And she also wrote short stories and children's books.

As for Jane/Jennie, she married Seth Delong after the closing date of this history. They had 2 children.

Jane E Wetherhorn
1914-1956

Spouse	**Seth D Delong**
Children	Catherine Mae Delong
	Francis Wayne Delong

Sophie Wetherhorn Deck
1873-1919

Spouse   Peter Sanford Deck

Sophie Wetherhorn was born on September 5th, 1873 in Augusta, GA. She grew up in the Wetherhorn home, where she was also in contact with her maternal grandfather and uncle. On June 25th, 1895, at age 22 she married Peter Sanford Deck, who usually went by the name Sanford. The newlyweds initially lived in her parents' house.

Sanford went to work for the Central of Georgia Railway. The couple moved to Savannah, and was living at 15 Liberty Street in 1907. Working for the Railway was a favored occupation at that time. Central of Georgia was probably the largest single employer in Savannah. We often forget what a massive impact the development of railroads had on the economy of the United States. Railroads were able to move large quantities of goods (and passengers) and had special cars for carrying the mail. Canal boats had limited access to the countryside. But railroads, once the track was laid, could go almost everywhere. Central of Georgia started long before the Civil War, but almost all of the company's track and rolling stock was destroyed during that conflict. New management rebuilt the railroad, changing to what is now standard gauge in the process. Soon Central of Georgia trains were travelling from Savannah to Chattanooga and across a web of rail lines that covered most of the middle of the state. Peter Sanford Deck became an engineer on their trains.

In 1908 and 1909 the Decks are recorded as living at 216 Liberty St. They also had another new convenience, a telephone, number 204. By 1914 they had moved to 315 Ogelthorpe, where they remained. They had a new telephone number, also, 1648J. Sanford stopped driving trains to become the roundhouse foreman for the large Central of Georgia yard in Savannah.

The couple did not enjoy this new arrangement for long. Sophie suffered from chronic Bright's disease which combined with heart failure to end her life on September 14th, 1919. She was buried in Bonaventure Cemetery, section K lot 392.

Sanford lived briefly with his in-laws. Then he remarried. His new wife, Ruth Zipperer, was about 20 years younger.

When he died in 1937 he was buried near Sophie. When Ruth died several years later, she was also buried in Bonaventure, but separately.

Arthur   Wetherhorn
1878-1954

Spouse   **F Silverstein**
Children   Eunice Wetherhorn   p. 75

Jules B Wetherhorn   p. 77

Zelda Wetherhorn   p. 78

David Wetherhorn   p. 80

Arthur was born in Swainsboro, Georgia on the last day of August, 1878. When he was 21 he is recorded as working at his father's general store in Waynesboro. At that time he was still single and living at home. The Savannah Georgia Health Officer's record shows his marriage to Fannye Silverstein in that city was reported on January 11th, 1908. *The Atlanta Constitution* edition of January 3rd, 1909 mentions the marriage of Arthur Wetherhahn to Fannye Silverstein of Savannah on page 3. The marriage took place at her home on January 12th. The reports both exhibit some common errors in spelling names. The family name was usually spelled Wetherhorn, and the bride spelled her name "Fannye".

War One. Since he was 40 years old, and had a family, he was not called.

By 1920 the family had grown to 5 and they were living at 310 Henry Street. The city had also grown by some 20,000 residents and now numbered over 80,000. As might be expected, the salary of the mayor also grew, from $3600 in 1910 to $6000 in 1920.

The family moved around a few times until about 1930 Arthur bought a permanent home. The house was valued at $7000 then. They also had a radio, a luxury that was not present in over half the homes in America at that time. It allowed them to listen to broadcasts like "Amos 'n Andy" a comic show about a pair of blacks in Harlem that were actually portrayed by 2 white actors.

Arthur and Fannye experienced one of the tragedies that many parents often fear. In 1938 their older son, Jules, was killed in a hunting accident. Details are in his chapter.

Arthur died on March 6th, 1954 and was buried in Bonaventure Cemetery , lot 558 section Q. Fannye died thirteen years later, on July 26th, 1967, and was laid to rest alongside him.

Arthur and Fannye Wetherhorn on the left visiting some of her family in Texas about 1934

Eunice Wetherhorn
1910-1965

Spouse	**Emanuel H Copeland**
Children	Anne Copeland
	Joan Copeland

Eunice Wetherhorn was born on Wednesday, December 22nd, 1909. The weather was fairly typical for Savannah at that time of year; light rain with a temperature of about 58 F. Weather observations at that time were being made from offices that had just been occupied in June of that year. They were located on the 9th floor of the National Bank Building at 41 Bull Street. The measurement instruments were on the roof of the building, about 150 feet above street level. The Weather Bureau occupied rooms 901, 902, 903, and 914.

In 1925 Eunice rated her own entry in the city directory that listed her with telephone number 1388. Eunice Married Emanuel Henry Copeland on September3rd, 1929, in the Mikve Israel congregation. The Mikve Israel building was constructed in 1878 and was designed in Gothic style, making it the only Jewish house of worship in America so designed. The newlyweds soon moved to Mobile Alabama. There Emanuel was employed as the manager of Kabers' shoe store at 121 Dauphine. They made their home at 116 ½ Glenwood.

By 1935 the Copelands had moved to Chattanooga, a larger city, where Emanuel was manager of the Vanity Boot Shop. They lived in Apt 6 at 921 Oak Street. Oak Street had several apartment buildings, but mostly only a few floors high. That was the same year that the game of Monopoly was invented. When it first went on sale it cost only one dollar. Emanuel apparently sought to improve his position and in 1937 he was a buyer for Lebeck Bros. Inc. a large Nashville department store. Their home was at 3901 Harding Road, Apt. 203.

While they were moving from place to place they found time to add 2 daughters to their family. Anne was born in Mobile on January 25th, 1933 and Joan was born in Nashville on July 8th, 1936.

By the end of the period covered in this history the family had moved once more. This time they were in Homewood City, an affluent suburb of Birmingham, Alabama. Their economic status was good enough for them to be able to have a live-in Negro maid.

Eunice died in 1965, her husband in 1967. They were buried in Elmwood Cemetery in Birmingham, AL.

Jules B Wetherhorn
1912-1938

Spouse   Dorothy Fine

Jules B. Wetherhorn was born on May 4th, 1912 in Savannah, Georgia. Since he had no children, I normally would have included him in his parents' chapter. But that section was already very long, so I decided to give him his own entry.

Jules, whose family nickname was "Bubba", went to Atlanta after high school, where he studied to become a dentist. In 1930 he was living at 430 Boulevard NE in apartment 1. While at the University of Georgia he met Dorothy Fine. She was also a student there, and a member of the Alpha Sigma Phi sorority. The two were married at Mikve Israel congregation in Savannah on September 1st, 1935. An item in *the Southern Israelite* on March 6th, 1936 mentions them as attending an event sponsored by the Alpha Omega dental fraternity.

They started out as a happy couple with lovely prospects, but all that came crashing down just a few days after their third anniversary. Jules went hunting for marsh hens with a good friend, Dr. Alex Paderewski of Savannah. The two men were in a boat near the South end of Wilmington Island. Jules fired at a bird and hit it. The bird fell in the water. The friends approached the dead bird in their boat and Jules tried to pick the bird out of the water. He laid down his automatic shotgun as he reached out. The gun was knocked off the seat and discharged. Jules was struck in the head by a load of birdshot and thrown off the boat. Dr. Paderewski pulled him back into the boat and went for help. County policeman B. W. Harper arrived and summoned an ambulance. Jules died about 10 minutes after reaching Savannah Hospital. Jules was buried the next day, September 12th, 1938 in Section Q lot 558 of Bonaventure Cemetery.

Dorothy later remarried.

Zelda Wetherhorn Homans
1914-1983

Spouse	**Jack Homans**
Children	Jules W Homans
	Lois Libby Homans
	Philip A Homans

Zelda Wetherhorn was born on October 8th, 1914 in Savannah, Georgia.

She was nearly 22 when she married Jack Homans. The couple was married at the home of Dr. and Mrs. Philip Rubin on East 39th St. Rita Slotin was Maid of Honor and only attendant. Peter Homansky, the groom's brother, was best man.

Jack had shortened his family name only a few years earlier. In 1930 he was still known as Jacob Homansky and was working at the Hole-in-the-Wall Shoe Store. Some people still called him Jake, but Jack was apparently the most used name.

After they married, Jack began looking for a better job. In 1938 he had found one as manager of the Vanity Slipper Shop in Raleigh, NC. The Vanity shops were a chain of stores with head offices in St. Louis, Missouri. They were in Raleigh when Jules, the first of their 3 children was born. In 1940 Jack had been promoted to managing the Vanity Slipper Shop at 117 S. Main in Greenville, SC.

Their home was at 604 Bennett in Greenville when Jack, standing 5 feet 10 ½ inches tall and weighing 155 pounds, registered for the draft.

At this point they crossed the limits of this family history. I will add that Jack died on April 13th, 1980, and Zelda followed on December 21st, 1983. They are both buried in Savannah's Bonaventure Cemetery.

David Wetherhorn
1920-1982

Spouse	J Jacobowitz
Children	Marc N Wetherhorn
	Nan Wetherhorn
	Amy Wetherhorn
	Ian Wetherhorn

David Wetherhorn was born on December 12th, 1920.

In 1920, when David was born, only about 1% of American homes had both electricity and indoor plumbing. Most of his life is outside the scope of this narrative.

When David was just 15 he had already been interested in astronomy. The family was living in Ways, Georgia, not far from the Bryan County estate of motor car magnate Henry Ford. During Ford's winter visit the two met and talked. Ford was impressed, and a few months later sent David a surprise gift, a 6 inch telescope. The gift got a brief mention in several newspapers.

Henry Ford was one of the wealthiest men in America. When automobiles were just beginning, in 1903, Some 11,235 were built in the USA. That same year 30,124 were built in France. Ford began building his cars on an assembly line in 1913. In the 1920s there were more cars in the state of Kansas than in the entire country of France. That year was when Chrysler and General Motors caught up with Ford in production.

It had started with Ford's 1908 model, the famous black Model T. The Model T sold for $290 in 1929. By that year about 32,028,000 automobiles had been made. Ninety per cent were made in the USA. Ford was paying his workers $5 per day.

David Wetherhorn studied chemical engineering at Vanderbilt University. After graduation he found temporary employment at the Calvert Distilling Company in Relay, Maryland. Relay is a smaller community that was created in

1830 as a relay point for the horses that pulled the early railroad cars before the introduction of steam engines. It is located in Baltimore County, just south of the University of Maryland. Calvert was headquartered in New York, but in 1934 established the branch in Relay. Originally they produced Calvert Whiskey, but today they just make alcohol.

David had grey eyes and brown hair. He was 5′ 8″ tall. He served in the army in World War Two. He later made a serious impact in the paper industry to the extent that an industry wide award was named in his honor.

He died in a scuba accident on January 5th, 1982.

Sarah Wetherhorn Kimball
1887-1965

Spouse	Oscar Alvin Kimball
Children	Hugh S Kimball p. 84
	Harry Oscar Kimball p. 84

Sarah Wetherhorn was born on February 27th, 1887, in Waynesboro, GA. She was about 21 when she married Oscar Alvin Kimball. The young couple lived in Savannah where he worked as a plumber. People knew him by his nickname, Duke. She was known as Sadie. Within a few years they had 2 sons, both born before the Great War in Europe. As far as I've been able to determine, he did not go overseas to fight, despite having been a member of the Georgia Militia for about 8 years. Possibly his family status was why he seems to have been left home.

The 1919 city directory lists them at 212 Hull St. with telephone number 4466. The national census the following year shows them renting a home at 224 State St.

The plumbing business went well. Oscar/"Duke" soon opened his own shop at 2518 Bull St. That was about 2 blocks north of the Atlantic Coast Line RR tracks. Sarah, whom according to her son, Patrick was called "Sadie", lived at home at 335 48th St., a similar distance south of the tracks. Their home phone number was now 5345 and they paid for a separate line for the business, number 6145. The post WWI boom helped them prosper even though Duke reportedly never went to school beyond the 6th grade. They bought the store property, and their home. As home owners and property owners they were now required to pay additional taxes to the City of Savannah, and they did. I found them both listed in the receipts registry of the city more than once. I suspect that the business was registered in his name, and their home in hers. Oscar also paid a separate city tax based on personal income.

The Kimballs allowed older son Hugh to have his own, independent, directory listing in 1928.

The Kimball family did move around a bit. It seems it was the plumbing office that moved most. I actually got the impression that there might have been 2 offices, but was unable to confirm this. O. A. Kimball became a heating and plumbing contractor. The business survived the great depression and even added jobs for family members. Their younger son, Harry Oscar Kimball, became the firm's sales manager in 1935, and Sarah's brother, Louie, was listed as a company employee since 1927.

When the Second World War broke out in Europe all the Kimballs decided to move further south, to Jacksonville, Florida. In 1943 the parents, Duke and Sadie, were living at 5213 Birkenhead Road in Jacksonville. Younger son Harry and his wife, Rose, were just down the street at 5243 Birkenhead. Harry was working at the St. Johns River Shipbuilding yard where my own father was also employed. They were constructing Liberty ships for the war effort. Older son Hugh and his wife Dorothy were also in Jacksonville, at 5225 Sunderland Road. Hugh was a salesman for Cameron and Barkley Co.

Oscar died in Jacksonville on May 29th, 1950. Sarah died there on October 30th, 1965. They are both buried in section H of Oaklawn Cemetery.

Hugh Kimball	
1911-1985	
Spouse	**Dorothy Mae Graw**
Children	Sarah D Kimball
	Dorothy Ann Kimball

Harry Kimball	
1913-1999	
Spouse	**Rosemary Coffey**
Children	Mary Anne Kimball
	Oscar Alvin Kimball
	Harry Henry Kimball
	Hugh A Kimball
	Patrick J Kimball

I am putting Hugh Solomon Kimball (born February 3rd, 1911 in Savannah) and Harry Oscar Kimball (born July 24th, 1913 in Savannah) in the same chapter.

They actually lived most of their lives after the 1940 cutoff date for this family history, and I've already mentioned a few things about them in the chapter about their parents.

Hugh continued as a student after high school and completed a degree as a civil engineer. He married Dorothy Mae Graw, usually called Dot, soon after. They were still in Savannah when their first daughter, Sarah Deborah, was born on October 18th, 1938.

They called her Debbie, possibly to avoid confusion with Hugh's mother.

When they moved to Jacksonville, FL, the following year Hugh found them accommodations in the Rochambeau Apartments at 2331 Riverside. They paid $45 a month for apartment #14 in the big building. His annual salary was $1400 from work in sales at a wholesale plumbing firm. That meant they were spending almost 1/3 of their income on housing.

In 1941 they moved to 1322 Donald St. That was the address given when Hugh registered for the draft. The draft board listed him as being 5'9" tall and weighing 160 pounds. His hair and eyes were both brown, and he wore glasses. But I've already strayed beyond the 1940 cut-off date. I'll just add that a second daughter was born in 1947. Hugh died on March 3rd 1985, and Dot followed him just 2 months later, on June 13th. They are both buried in Jacksonville's Oaklawn Cemetery.

Younger brother Harry only moved to Jacksonville when his parents made the change. His draft registration shows him as being slightly taller (5' 10") and lighter (155 pounds) than Hugh. He married Rosemary Coffey, who was 3 years his junior. Harry and Rosemary raised 5 children, all born after the closing date of this history.

He died in Jacksonville on May 19th, 1999. She survived him by more than a decade, dying on February 23rd, 2010. They are also both buried in Oaklawn Cemetery.

Louis L Wetherhorn
1889-1977

Spouse   Addie V Hinely

Children   Sophie Wetherhorn

Louie L. Weatherhorn was born April 4th, 1889, in Waynesboro GA. I found his name spelled in several ways. The family name appears most often as "Weatherhorn", but his first name can be seen as "Louie", "Louis", "Lewie" and "Lewis" in different places. In 1910, after their mother had died 2 years earlier, only he, his sister Bertha, and his brother Adolph were still at home with their father. Both boys worked in the family store. Around 1912 he married Addie V. Hinely. She was almost his age and had been born in rural Effingham County, which in those days was located just north of Savannah. I'm not certain, but believe that it is possible she was named for Valilia A. Hinely who died shortly before Addie's birth and is buried in the Jerusalem Lutheran Church Cemetery in Rincon, Effingham County, Georgia. The 1912 Savannah city directory shows Addie as working at Alexander Bros. in Savannah and living at 551 York.

The 1915 Savannah city directory has Louie Wetherhorn married to Addie, working at the Savannah Brewery, and living with his father, his brother, Adolph, and Adolph's wife Viola at 315 W. Oglethorpe. A separate entry, using the Weatherhorn spelling, has them living at 546 York, not far from where she had been living earlier. Louie and Addie's only child was born on November 19th, 1914. They named her Sophie Valilia Wetherhorn.

Louie registered for the draft in June, 1917. He was listed as being of medium height, slender, with dark brown eyes and hair. He was also listed as being exempt due to his being married and having a child. By the next year they had moved to 1833 W.

Broad St. Louie seems to have continued operating a soda water bottling machine for the Savannah Beverage and Ice Co. But the following year he was listed as working for Terry's. Louie seems to have tired of that job and learned plumbing. After they moved, once again, this time to 515 41st St., he began employment as a plumber for Seckinger and Garwes Plumbing and Heating located at 448 Drayton. In 1925 they left Savannah for a brief stay in West Palm Beach, FL where Louie was employed as a plumber by W. Krumpke. Eventually, back in Savannah, Louie went to work for his brother-in-law Oscar Kimball.

I thought it interesting to note that Addie was paying personal income tax to the City of Savannah but Louie was not listed. They were back living at 515 41st. in 1929. It was a rented home that cost them $14.50 every month. Now, almost a century later, you cannot rent a single room for more than ten times that amount.

Louie died on December 9th, 1977. Addie died on June 16th 1986. They buried together in Section M, lot 326, of Bonaventure Cemetery in Savannah.

Sophie, meanwhile, had grown into an attractive young woman. She married Loy Wymond Crapps, He was just starting out as a plumber. Sadly, on February 4th, 1939, he was involved in an automobile accident. This was an era long before seat belts in cars. Loy suffered a broken neck and died. Sophie later remarried. Her new husband was Claude Alfred Schunneman. His family came from Germany, but they were not Jewish. Sophie was a member of the Trinity Methodist Church. She was buried in Bonaventure Cemetery. I've included this because there is a headstone in that cemetery with the names "Crapps" and "Wetherhorn" engraved on it. Loy is buried there. Sophie is buried at a different site in the same cemetery, alongside Claude Schunneman.

Adolph   Wetherhorn
1891-1972

Spouse   Viola May Riley

Spouse   Inez Burke

Adolf Wetherhorn has a very short chapter. I almost combined him with his parents because he had no children. But that's getting ahead of the story. He was born in Waynesboro on September 9th, 1891. He worked in his father's store when he was younger. He also managed to put in 4 years' service as a private in the state National Guard. In 1913 He married Viola May Riley. Everyone called her "Vi". The couple lived at various addresses in Savannah, GA. He worked as an electrician and she was a saleswoman, and later a department head, at Adler's. I have no record of a divorce, but it seems that did occur at some time before 1955. They had no children.

The city directories for 1955 and 1960 show Adolph married to Inez Burke. In those years he worked as a salesman for Crown Motor Company. Adolph died on December 24th, 1972 in Savannah and Inez on September 13th, 1981. They are buried side by side in Bonaventure Cemetery in Savannah. Viola remarried. I found her with her 2nd husband, Robert O. Dunning, in Savannah in 1951. I did not find a record of their marriage. She died in Braidwood, Illinois, on January 6th, 1981 and was buried 4 days later in Bonaventure Cemetery under the name Viola May Dunning. Her grave is next to that of Robert O. Dunning in lot 39 block C section 11.

The main reason I kept Adolf in a separate chapter was to have space to address the issue of Jewish assimilation. The original 5 Wetherhorn brothers all married. Four of them found Jewish girls. But the next generation was different. Obviously, none of Abraham's children remained Jewish. It's doubtful if Philip's 2 sons did because I found no mention of them anywhere. Levy

had a better record. Four of the six of his children that married
had Jewish spouses. Solomon had the worst record. Only one of
his children, Arthur, married another Jew. In other words, there
were a great many of the descendants of Marcus Wetherhorn who
were successful in integrating into the majority religion in
America. There is no official program to make Jews abandon
their religion in America like the programs and pogroms that
occurred in Europe. Those that retained their Jewish identity
seem to have a highly disproportionate effect on their country.
American Jews make up a mere 2 per cent of the total
population. A scan of almost any record of influential
individuals in any field in the United States will almost certainly
show a percentage of Jews greater than 2. But, as you can see in
this book, maintaining a link to a Jewish religion is not always a
high priority for many of them. The Jewish religion says that
religious identity is passed down via the mother. On my own
mother's side, there are 12 first cousins. Nine have Jewish
spouses. On my father's side the split is about 50-50. There are
many reasons why an individual may want to keep his
religious/cultural identity. There are probably just as many that
work in the opposite direction. I don't have any answers here. But
I do want to say that there will likely be people who are
mentioned here whose descendants will be surprised to learn
that they have Jewish ancestors.

Bertha Wetherhorn Hall
1893-1969

Spouse   **Amos Sylvanus Hall**

Children   Lena Elizabeth Hall   p. 93

Sanford Hall   p. 94

Solomon Hall   p. 95

Evelyn Talmadge Hall   p. 96

Adolph Roy Hall   p. 96

Hinton Eve Hall   p. 97

Francis Arnold Hall   p. 97

Patricia Ann Hall   p. 98

baby girl Hall
Gloria L Hall   p. 99

Bertha Wetherhorn was born on November 28th, 1893. She was just 15 years old when she embarked upon a great adventure. She tried to elope with the family chauffer, Amos Sylvanus Hall. Amos was 5 years older than Bertha. He was reported as being of medium height and build, but he appears tall in the photograph of the two of them together because she was quite short.

Amos had an interest in the early automobiles and turned that interest into a profession. He worked as a driver for the Wetherhorn family and others. He actually resided in the Wetherhorn home in Waynesboro in 1910 along with Solomon, Louie, Adolph and Bertha. That may have been where the romance began.

In late 1910 Amos and Bertha plotted to elope to Augusta and get married there. They left the family home and embarked on a train to Augusta. But somehow, word of their plans became known. Bertha's father telephoned the police in Augusta. When the eloping couple arrived they were met by the local cops. Bertha was escorted back to her family in Waynesboro. Amos was detained, briefly, in Augusta, before being released. Bertha was sent to Savannah to visit her sister. When she returned after a few weeks the two of them maintained proper relations, even to the extent of not greeting each other when they met. But that wasn't the end of the story.

In February 1911 Amos was working as a chauffeur for a Captain W. A. Wilkins. He drove his employer, and a companion, Mr. W. C. Hillhouse, to Augusta in an automobile belonging to Capt. Wilkins. Amos inquired how long it would be before he was needed again and was told that his passengers would probably take about 3 hours to finish the business that brought them to Augusta. That was enough time. Amos drove quickly back to Waynesboro, picked up Bertha, and returned to Augusta. This time Mr. James Garvin Hall, Amos's father, was waiting with a preacher and a marriage license. They returned to Waynesboro as Mr. and Mrs. Amos Hall.

Amos Hall soon found employment in Savannah as a machinist at Thomas Bryson's automobile garage. He and Bertha moved to Savannah. By June, when Amos registered for the First World War draft, they already had 2 offspring, a girl and a boy. Their second son was born that same month. That may have kept him out of the Army. More children followed. Most their lives are not included

here because they all come after the 1940 cut-off date for this his- tory. Some do have separate short chapters but one merits a special mention here.

On November 11th, 1935, Bertha went to Warren Candler Hospital to give birth. The baby, a girl, survived only one day. As far as I know she was never given a name. The death certificate says she succumbed to a brain hemorrhage. The body was given to Sipple's Funeral home and buried in Laurel Grove Cemetery.

The hospital is also worth a brief note. It was the oldest hospital in Savannah. In 1931 Asa Griggs Candler endowed the hospital and had it renamed Warren Candler Hospital in honor of his brother. Asa Griggs Candler was the man who purchased the recipe for Coca Cola in 1888. He established the Coca Cola Company four years later and turned it into what is probably the best known brand name in the world. The hospital was founded in 1804, long before the endowment, and is one of the two hospitals in America with the longest records of continuous operation.

Now, we return to our heroes. Amos seemed unable to settle down at a single job or remain in a single home for very long. The family, which continued to grow, moved from house to house while Amos bounced from job to job. They tried moving to West Palm Beach in Florida in 1930, possibly because of the Great Depression. The rented home there cost them $25 a month. By 1932 they were back in Savannah. The place they rented in 1935 cost only $10 per month, another symptom of the broken economy. Amos died on November 9th, 1943. He was buried in Hillcrest Abbey East Cemetery. Bertha moved to 531 Garden Homes. She died on February 12th, 1969 and was laid to rest alongside her husband.

Lena Elizabeth Hall
1913-1990

Spouse   **Ralph M Edwards**

Children   Peggy Jean Edwards

Lena Elizabeth Hall was born on March 23rd, 1913. By the time she was a teen-ager America was in the grip of The Great Depression. She found a job for a short while as a laundress in a steam laundry. It did not last long. By 1930 she had been unemployed for an entire year.

Lena married Ralph Mitchell Edwards, two years her senior, on January 29th, 1933. He was from South Carolina and they were married in Jasper County, SC. Jasper County is located just across the Savannah River to the north of Savannah. The marriage was performed by Leland Stanley McCormack. McCormack was a hardware merchant who also served as the county probate judge.

An interesting sidelight about Stanley McCormack is that he and a partner opened the first movie theater in Jasper County. It screened early silent films, but for only 3 days of every week. Early movie theaters were often called Nickelodeons because the admission price was usually 5 cents.

Lena and Ralph remained in Savannah. Their only child, daughter Peggy Jean, was born there on August 16th, 1929. Lena died on April 21st, 1980 and was buried in Hillcrest Abbey East. Ralph did not die until July 25th, 1996. He is buried next to his wife.

Sanford Hall
1915-1983

Spouse	**Corabelle Chiles**	
Children	Kenneth	Hall
	Richard Stanford Hall	
	Brenda Evette Hall	
	Donald Edward Hall	
	Debra Belle Hall	

Sanford Hall was born in Waynesboro on February 16th, 1915.

He married Corabelle Chiles on March 3rd, 1940 across the state line in South Carolina. Probate judge Mc Cormack, who had performed his sister Lena's marriage, officiated. The Couple initially lived with her mother and stepfather while Sanford worked as an auto mechanic at the Jackson Motor Co. located at 218 E. Broughton. Their first child, Richard, was born before the cutoff for this family history. They had 4 more children. The picture below shows them with their granddaughter, Christa Louise Sloan.

Sanford died on May 17th, 1983 and Cora on September 4th 1985. They are buried in Greenwich Cemetery. He is in lot 25 block Q section 9 and she is in section 7.

Solomon Hall
1917-1969

Spouse   **Mildred Mingledorf**

Children   Pamela Virginia Hall

               Richard Sol Hall

Solomon Hall was born in Savannah, Georgia on June 10th 1917. He may have learned a lot about automobiles from his father. Real changes in his life came just at the edge of the period covered in this family history. Solomon, who was known as Sol, married Mildred Virginia Mingledorff on June 9th, 1940.

She had been living with her sister in Savannah and working as a salesgirl in a department store. After they were married, Sol and Minky, as she was known, moved to Charlotte, NC. He started working as a mechanic for DeWitte Motor Company, but soon moved to join the crew at Bob Robinson Auto. He also registered with the Selective Service. At the time, he was 5'6" tall and weighed 175 pounds. The local draft board did not call him to serve until November, 1942. Minky moved to a smaller apartment while Sol was in the Army. He served as an artillery section chief with the 532nd Ordnance Bn. He finished the war as a Tech. Sgt., was released on December 12th, 1945, and returned home to the same job he had before the war. The couple later had 2 children.

Sol died of a heart attack on Thursday, May 22nd, 1969. He was buried in Evergreen Burial Park, Mint Hill, Charlotte, NC, two days later. Mildred survived him by 27 years. She died on October 6th, 1996 and was buried alongside him 2 days later.

The next one of Bertha and Amos Hall's children was born on March 3rd, 1920. She was named Evelyn Talmadge Hall. In common with all her subsequent siblings, the majority of important event in her life took place outside the date range covered here.

Spouse	**Herbert F Chellette**
Children	Linda E Chelette
	Jeanette Chellette
	Herbert L Chellette

Adolph Roy Hall
1923-2005

Spouse	**Mary Lillian Lott**
Children	Mary Ellen Hall
	Paulette Ann Hall
	Johnnie Margaret Hall
	Donna Lou Hall
	Nancy Sue Hall
	David Roy Hall
	Kay Louise Hall
	Lisa Marie Hall

She was married to Herbert Foster Chelette. They are both buried in Mt Zion Cemetery in Louisiana.

That brings us to Adolf Roy Hall who was born on March 9th, 1923.

I have one lovely story about him that I feel I must include despite the fact that it occurs outside the date range.

I got this from his granddaughter, Melanie Amacker:

"My Grand Daddy name was Adolph Roy Hall. He was born March 9th, 1923.

He originally did not have a middle name but due to the happenings of WWII. He did not want his initials to match the evil leader. He didn't want to change his name completely so Roy became his middle name. My Grand Daddy didn't even tell my Grandmother his real name at first because he heard her talking about how she hated the name Adolf Hitler. When she asked his name, he replied, Johnny , which she affectionately called him.

"She called him Adolph only when it was serious. He served in WWII, Korea, and Vietnam as an Army medic".

One detail Melanie left out was that he met his future wife at a USO dance, and that was where he told her his name was "Johnny". They married and raised eight girls. Oh, Yes, up to his death, everyone knew him as Johnny Hall.

The remaining 4 children on Amos and Bertha were all still teen-agers, or younger, when the period covered ended. I am listing them here just for completeness and without spelling out any of their history. Their names were; Hinton Eve Hall, Francis Arnold Hall, Patricia Ann Hall (known as Pattyann"), and Gloria L Hall.

Hinton Eve Hall was born on July 10th, 1925 and died on February 13th, 2001

Hinton Eve Hall
1923-2005

Spouse	**Beulah Lee Worth**
Children	Kathy Hall
	Larry Daniel Hall
	Barbara Ann Hall
	Robyn Hall
	Thomas Claude Hall

Francis Arnold Hall
1927-2008

Spouse	**Dorothy Mae Allen**
Children	James A Hall
	Cheryl Elaine Hall

Francis Arnold Hall was born on June 17th, 1927 and died on August 11th, 2008.

Patricia Ann Hall
1932-2013

Spouse	**Christy Dubois**
Children	Christy Dubois Jr
	Walter Daniel Dubois
	Janice Diane Dubois
	Randall Amos Dubois
	Ronald S Dubois

Patricia Ann Hall was born on January 26th, 1932 and died on March 23rd, 2013.

Gloria L Hall
1938-Living

Spouse   **Autry Mayo Farris**

Spouse   **Leslie E Purdee**

Children   Leslie Michael Purdee

            Timothy Lee Purdee

Gloria L. Hall was born on April 11th, 1938.

Levi Wetherhorn
1842-1910

Spouse	P Pincussohn
Children	Sophia Wetherhorn
	Hannah Wetherhorn p. 109
	Leopold Wetherhorn p. 114
	Jenette Wetherhorn p. 144
	Sadie Wetherhorn p. 147
	Marcus Wetherhorn
	Gabriel Wetherhorn p. 149
	Henry Wetherhorn p. 149
	Mitchell Wetherhorn p. 149
	Hermine Wetherhorn p. 152

5
Levi Wetherhorn

Levy Wetherhorn (sometimes spelled Levi) was born on June 16th 1842. He was the first of the family to be born in the United States. He was born the same year that the Old Croton Aqueduct was completed in New York. It was the first location in the US to provide constant water pressure for the city fire mains and was also expected to aid in controlling cholera. I suspect that Levy was more outgoing than his brothers. The 1850 US Census shows them living in the Parish of St.  Phillip and St. Michaels. Those were two prominent churches not far from their home. Street names had existed for a long time, but house numbers were not uniform. The city council commissioned a man to make order out of the numbering system in 1858, with the hope that it would be complete before the 1860 census. Levy was just a few days shy of his 13th birthday when his mother died of cholera. Two years later his father remarried. His new stepmother had only been in the United States a short while. The boys from the first marriage may have been uncomfortable with her presence. They did, for whatever reason, begin to move out of the old family home. Levy began working as an apprentice to a carpenter. He also joined the City Militia. He was a member of the German Riflemen. This would soon give him a ringside seat to an important event in American history.

The political crisis over slavery was becoming more intense. When states, led by South Carolina, declared they were seceding from the Union. Many residents who did not support slavery continued to support their home states. The Governor of South Carolina called up the militia for 90 days, and included Charleston's German Riflemen. The company, commanded by CAPT Jacob Small, provided security for the artillery battery on Morris Island. The guns were manned by Citadel cadets. They opened fire on Fort Sumter.

When the 90 day call up ended, Levi joined battery A of the 1st SC artillery. The battery was also known as Wegener's battery, after the commander, CAPT F. W. Wegener. It was also called the German light artillery because of the origin of many of the men. Most of Levi's brothers would also serve in this unit. The battery spent almost the entire war facing off the Federal blockading squadron that isolated Charleston from the outside world. A Federal army landed on the coast and approached Charleston from the north. They were unable to cross the river, so contented themselves with bringing in heavy artillery and bombarding the city. There was a lot of damage. Near the end of the war Levi was away from the battery, foraging for food, when he was captured by a Federal patrol. He was briefly imprisoned in Fort Sumter after the confederate forces in Charleston had evacuated the city. He was paroled and the war ended soon after. He remained in contact with other veterans and that was the basis for my mother saying he was a civil war general. Okay, he wasn't a general. But the idea started me on a wonderful voyage of discovery about a lot of people

Levi went back to carpentry. In 1867 He married Pena Pinckus (sometimes spelled Pincussohn). The 1870 US Census shows them living in Ward 6 in Charleston with their oldest child, Sophia. She was born on November 27th, 1867. More children followed. The fourth child, a boy, was born on February 14th, 1876. He was named Marcus after his grandfather who had died almost 3 years earlier. I mention these two specifically because they do not have chapters of their own. Sophia came down with typhoid fever at the end of November, 1882. Her condition worsened and she died on December 16th of that year. She was just 15 years old.

Marcus survived a bout with whooping cough in 1880, as did his younger brother Gabriel. Whooping cough was often a fatal childhood disease in that era. Marcus was confirmed at Congregation Kahal Kadosh Beth Elohim (KKBE) on June 7th, 1890. His sister Jenette (Nettie) was also one of the 15 members of the confirmation class. The Reverend David Levy, leader of the Reform Temple, spoke. The event was reported in *The American Israelite* newspaper the following week, including the full text of Rev. Levy's speech. Sadly, Marcus only survived that event by a couple of years. He was riding in a truck near 14 Globe Street in Charleston on March 30th, 1892, when he was accidentally thrown to the street. He died from his injuries. Marcus and Sophia were buried together in the KKBE Huguenin Ave cemetery.

Levi, meanwhile, had been actively working to achieve a better life for himself and his family. He is recorded as working for Toale Mfg. in 1875. He had joined the company as a carpenter. Patrick P. Toale had established his company as a premier supplier of doors, sashes, and blinds in the region. He had sales offices and show rooms at 20-22 Hayne and at 33-35 Pinckney. The manufacturing hall was on Fort near Broad.

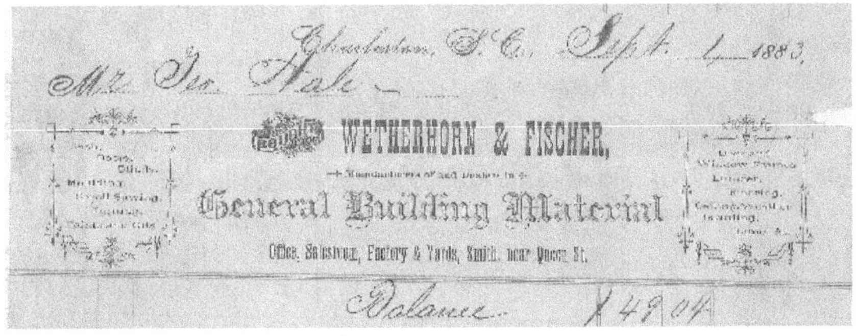

Levi soon established himself as a capable and knowledgeable worker. In 1877 the Toale advertisement in the city directory even listed him, by name, as the manager of the factory and yards. Levi was learning all aspects of the business.

Making contacts on the social side was also not neglected. Levy joined the local B'nai Brith lodge. He was elected warden of Dan Lodge #93 I.O.B.B. in 1871. The standing of the family can also be judged from the 1880 US Census. It shows Levy and his wife with 7 children at 91 Broad Street. It also shows they had domestic help. There are three servants listed; Linda Watterhouse, aged 53, plus Cinda Wright and Martha Lafitte. The last two are both blacks and both aged 40. It seems Levy weathered the recession of 1873-1876 reasonably well.

In 1879 Levi still worked at Toale's and lived at 91 Broad St. That location became the site where the US Court House and Post Office was built in 1896. But Levi had been talking with another German immigrant named Augustus Fischer. Everything would soon change. The city directory of 1883 showed Levi working at E. W. Percival's, a competitor of Toale. The family was now temporarily residing at 338 King Fischer and Wetherhorn became partners and prepared to open their own lumber yard and sash manufacturing business. The new yard was located on Smith Street. It took up the entire block from number 7 to number 13. I have an original copy of one of the earliest receipts (shown on p. 103).Notice the date: September 1st, 1883. Two months later Augustus Fischer would marry Matilda Cappell at his home on 36 Church Street.

It was interesting to me to notice that the 1883 Shole's city directory carried a large, half page, advertisement for Wetherhorn and Fischer. I've included it here. There was a smaller ad on an earlier page from E. W.

Percival. But there was no ad from Toale. According to the publisher's notes, the directory was prepared in February, 1883. At that time, the population of the city was just over 56,909.

The business prospered. I found several ads in the local area newspapers. Some of them were seeking additional employees to work in the yard.

In 1884 Levy and his family were living at 409 King Street. It was a 4 ½ story building built in 1808 and later purchased for the Aimar Pharmacy. The upper stories became the Aimar House Hotel.

Natural disasters soon came along to disrupt life in Charleston. In 1885 the city was hit by a massive hurricane. Today it would be classified as a category 2 storm, with winds of about 100 mph and a surge of water that flooded the lower parts of the city. Water was even reported as flowing UP Meeting Street.

This is a picture of the South Battery after the storm. Notice the boat that has been tossed inland over the seawall.

The following year, 1886, Charleston was the site of a very rare natural disaster, an earthquake. It struck just before 10:00 PM on August 31st. Measuring about 7.6 on today's Richter scale, it was one of the most severe earthquakes ever recorded on the American Eastern

Seaboard. Some 100 people were killed. The damage was extensive. An estimated 14,000 chimneys were toppled. Most structures in the city were reported as being damaged. The value of the damage was estimated as being over $5,000,000. That would be around $112,000,000 today. The picture at the bottom of the previous page was taken the morning after and shows the damage at the corner of Cumberland and East Bay.

Rebuilding after these tragedies was obviously beneficial to building suppliers like the lumber yard.

In 1889 the family was living at 10 Greene Street in one of a pair of 2 story tenements constructed in Greek revival style in 1841. Today only one survives; the other was destroyed to make room for relocating the house at 6 Greene Street.

1889 was also a year of major expansion for Wetherhorn and Fischer. The lumber business had become one of the largest in the South. When the yard was first opened the clientele was mostly local planters and builders. By 1889 lumber exports had become a truly big deal in South Carolina. Northern pine had earlier been imported for construction work. But there was another indigenous tree that was largely overlooked, the cypress. Cypress was found in abundance in the swamps of lowland South Carolina. However, most cypress was cut and then used fairly quickly. Northern pine had been dried and aged before being imported for construction in the South. Wetherhorn and Fischer reasoned, correctly, that if local cypress could be properly dried to avoid warpage it could be a superior, more durable, and cheaper, alternative. They imported a large drying kiln for that purpose. It was installed in their lumber yard. The drying process took only 24 hours. Soon cypress became one of the leading products and a component of many locally manufactured wooden products such as furniture as well as a staple for building construction.

1889 was also the year the company got a telephone. The number was 309, making it one of the earlier telephones in the city. The first telephone exchange had actually been installed on the second floor at 1 Broad Street nearly 10 years earlier. At that

time the number of subscribers was still very small and the
spread of lines connecting other parts of the city did not seem
too rapid.

Levy moved family to a new home on 10 Green Street. The
house was big enough to also accommodate some added
family members. His daughter, Hannah, married Samuel Link
and the young couple resided in her parents' house. The other
older children who had married were no longer living at
home.

Elzas' book about Jewish life in Charleston mentions the
Wetherhorns as prominent merchants.

In 1891 the firm got a brief bit of bad press when one of the
colored workers, (the yard apparently did not practice
discrimination in hiring) a man named Willie Davis, got his hand
caught in some of the machinery. He was unable to get free, and
the hand was severed at the wrist. A Charleston police ambulance
took him to the hospital. I was unable to locate any follow up to
this story which was printed in the *Manning Times.*

The 1897 directory still shows the family at 10 Green Street.
They were next door to A. J. Myers and only 2 houses away
from Mrs. Hannah Triest. Mrs. Rosa Tobias had her home in the
next block. In terms of location, they were in the center of the
Charleston Jewish Community. It may have been around this
time that the Wetherhorn family acquired a permanent pew in the
main hall of KKBE. The brass plate that still identifies it, however,
probably dates from a slightly later era.

Leopold, the oldest son, took up an assignment as bookkeeper
for the firm. By 1903 he was listed as a full partner along with his
father and Mr. Fischer. In 1903 the family moved to a new home
at 123 Wentworth, almost across the street from the homes of
the Louis Cohen and Ottolenghi families. Soon Levy would move
across the street and leave the house at 123 to his son.

On January 28th, 1910, Levy Wetherhorn died from heart failure. He had lived the American dream. Starting as the son of a small immigrant shopkeeper, he had learned carpentry and made that into a one of the largest manufacturing facilities for wooden doors and lumber in the entire region.

His wife, Pena, officially inherited the business. But the real direction of the firm passed on to his son, Leopold. Pena died on January 25th, 1915 and was laid to rest in the family plot of the Huguenin Ave. Cemetery. The inscription on the monument above them reads "In life loving and beloved, In death not divided".

Leopold donated new stained glass windows to Temple KKBE in memory of his parents and maternal grandparents. Those windows are still there in the main sanctuary just to the right of the podium. A color version is on the cover.

Hannah   Wetherhorn
1870-1946

Spouse   **Samuel Herman Link**

Children   Sadie Josephine Link

Hannah Wetherhorn was born in Charleston on June 4th, 1870. When she was 20 years old she married Samuel Herman Link. The KKBE Rabbi, Reverend David Levy, conducted the ceremony on September 7th, 1890.

The Links started in Orangeburg, a few miles to the North. Later they lived with her parents at 10 Green St. Sam Link worked as a drummer (a traveling salesman). Their first child, daughter Sadie Josephine, was born on February 12th, 1891. She died while still an infant, on January 26th, 1892.

Charleston had long ago organized several Jewish communal self-help societies. In 1901 The Hebrew Benevolent Society operated under the presidency of Montagu Triest. He was also the secretary-treasurer of the Hebrew Orphan Society. There was even a Hebrew Ladies Sewing Society run by Miss Annie Solomon at that time.

Sam Link became ill and died at 8 PM on May 9th, 1907 in the Charleston Riverside Infirmary. He was only 44 years old. Hannah was left to raise their 2 sons. She initially remained at their home at 162 E. Russell in Orangeburg, but soon moved back to Charleston where she stayed with her mother. In 1915 she decided to move to New York. Her home became a home away from home for many of the family. In 1920 her brother Gabriel lived with her. In 1925 she shared her home with Fannie Wald, the daughter of her late husband's sister, Lena. In 1940 her son Sol and his wife and son lived with her. My own father stayed with her when he attended Columbia University.

Hannah was not a quiet and withdrawn individual. She was also active in the National Council of Jewish Women. Her life in NY included the era of prohibition, and the period of many of the famous American criminals. The Federal Bureau of Investigation was created in 1907, but didn't become a legend until J. Edgar Hoover took over as director in 1924. During the period of his directorship the FBI apprehended and helped convict Al Capone of Chicago. The most important criminal that Hoover brought down was probably John Dillinger. Dillinger's gang robbed 24 banks and 4 police stations. He had escaped from prison and was personally responsible for killing one police officer before law enforcement agents caught up with him at last. Dillinger was killed in a shootout with them in Chicago in 1934.

Hannah Died on last day of December, 1946 in Manhattan. But she is buried in the Charleston KKBE Huguenin Ave Cemetery.

Solomon Link
1893-1984

Spouse	**Lilian Friedman**
Children	Sanford Alfred Link

Solomon Link was born in Charleston on June 10th, 1893. He was probably named after his grandfather who had died a couple of years earlier. His father died in 1907. Sol soon went to work as a clerk in the I. M. Pearlstine and sons' grocery business. I always felt this was just a sign of how the Jewish community in Charleston was quite close. Sol's cousin, Sophie Wetherhorn, would later marry Leo Pearlstine, the grandson of the company founder. Sol remained employed at Pearlstine's until the family moved to New York in 1915.

In New York, Solomon found work in sales and quickly rose to be head of the hosiery department.

Then the US entered the war. Sol was inducted into the army and given serial number 780258. After basic training at Fort Slocum he embarked on a transport and headed for France. He was in France from June 6th, 1918 until October 12th, 1919. He served with the Supply Company of the 309th QMC. He was advanced in rank to private first class in April, 1919. As a member of the Quartermasters Corps he did not spend time in combat in the trenches, but that fact also lowered his priority for receiving orders to go home. Sol returned to the US from Brest, France, on board the USS GREAT NORTHERN in October, 1919. He was discharged on October 18th, 1919 after spending about 22 months in the Army.

Sol returned to work in sales and lived with his mother and brother until he met a young stenographer named Lillian Friedman. She was 20 years old when they married in Manhattan on March

20th, 1923. The marriage took place just 3 weeks after the first edition of *Time* magazine hit the newsstands. The couple rented an apartment on West 165th Street for $85 per month. They were living there when their only child was born. Her father, a widower, moved in with them for a while. Later they would move in with his mother when she was not hosting any other family members.

Their son, Sanford Alfred Link, was born on April 20th, 1927. He was still a child when the limiting date of this history was reached. I am going to mention that he married Susan Abolafia in 1953 but anything else is outside the scope of this volume.

Solomon Link died on November 6th, 1984 and was buried in Flushing, NY.

Marcus Emile Link
1899-1962

Spouse   **Sally Bader**

Children   Patricia Bette Link

Marcus Emile Link was born in Charleston on June 2nd, 1899. Shortly after his birth the first Hague Conference convened. The Hague Conventions regarding the conduct of war that emerged from that conference are regarded as the foundation of International Law with regard to War. That is true despite the fact that many of the provisions of those conventions were disregarded during the First World War by nations that had accepted and even ratified them.

Marcus lived with his mother and brother. In 1914 he was employed as a clerk at Wilbur's Arcade Cigar Store in Charleston. After the family moved to NY the following year, and while he was still a student, he began work at Commerce Investment Trust. He remained an employee, and later an executive, at this company until his death.

On March 1st, 1932, he married Sally Bader in Manhattan. Their daughter, Patricia, was born in 1935. The glasses he always wore might have obscured his grey eyes. He was 5' 7" tall, and being over 40, married, and with a young child, the combination was probably enough to keep him from being drafted into the Army in World War II.

Sally died on November 14th, 1962. Her husband preceded her in death on July 10th, 1954.

Leopold Wetherhorn
1872-1926

Spouse   **Rosalie Zerline Kahn**

Children   Sophie Z Wetherhorn p. 118

My Grandfather, Leopold Wetherhorn, was born in Charleston on November 23rd, 1867. As soon as he was old enough to work he joined his father at the lumber yard and manufacturing plant on Smith Street. He grew with the facility. Soon he became the firm's accountant. When Augustus Fischer left, the company became L. Weatherhorn and Son. Leopold was the son.

I found a newspaper article in the June 24th, 1891 edition of the *Watchman and Southron* from Sumter, South Carolina. It mentions that the annual distribution hop took place in the Armory there. For those who might not be familiar with the term, a hop was a term used then for a dance where contemporary popular music was played, as opposed to a ball, which was more formal and tended toward music and dances from an earlier era. The article mentioned that the hop (dance) was given annually to mark the end of the social season. The article went on to mention many of the participants at this specific hop. Among those mentioned were Julius Wetherhorn, Nettie Wetherhorn, Leo Wetherhorn, and Rosa Kahn.

Almost 6 years later, on March 16th, 1897 Leopold married Rosalie Zerline Kahn. The marriage took place in New York. Later, a stained glass window would be installed in the passage from the main sanctuary of KKBE to the adjacent Barbara Pearlstine social hall. The names of Leopold and Rosa, and the date of their wedding are part of that window. The ability to donate that window, and others items that will be mentioned later was a symbol of how well the company was doing financially.

Another item pointing to the higher standing in the Jewish community that the Wetherhorn family enjoyed at that time was a mention in a letter from my aunt, Sophie Wetherhorn Pearlstine, which recalled that both Levy and Leopold had served terms as president of the KKBE congregation. One of the things that excited me when I visited the KKBE building was to see the large stained glass windows on the side of the pulpit. The KKBE building had been damaged by the Charleston earthquake of 1886. The structure was intact, but many windows had been shattered. My grandfather made a donation to pay for the two

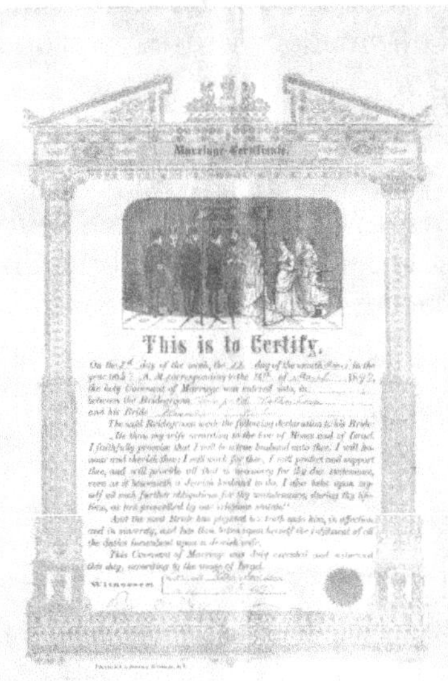

Leopold and Rosalie Wetherhorn and their children about 1920

Their marriage certificate called a Ketuba in Jewish Law

windows on the right side as you face the altar. One of them commemorates his parents. The other is in honor of my grandmothers parents. Their names appear in the glass at the lower edge of the windows. When I last visited, the pew that my family had occupied regularly was still marked with a brass

plate with the family name. The last male Wetherhorn to use it was my uncle Leo, who died in 1987.

These pictures show the lower part of the windows and the pew. I used only the bottom of the windows so the names would show. The smaller picture gives an indication of how high they really are.

Many relatives outside his own family called my grandfather "Bubba". His cousin Rufus, the son of Abraham Wetherhorn, was also known by the same nickname. Some others called him "Henry". Leopold took over the family business and employed several of his own children in various jobs. The business was a successful one. But then a disaster struck. Around Dec 25th, 1925, (I haven't found a confirmation for the exact date) there was a fire at the lumber yard. The entire facility was destroyed. My father told me it might have been set by a disgruntled employee, but there was no proof of that, either. Whatever the cause, the Charleston Fire Department was not able to quench the inferno before everything was consumed by the flames. There was insurance. According to Arthur Williams, who was married to Zerline Levy, the daughter of Leopold's sister in law, Fannie, Leopold decided to invest the money in a shipment of illegal whiskey. The US Coast Guard intercepted the shipment and Leopold then shot himself. I found a death certificate that does not agree with that story. The official file says Leopold died from an accidental ingestion of rat poison on March 1st, 1926. Leopold suffered for 7 days before he died. The certificate was signed by Dr. Kivvy Pearlstine. Kivvy was THE Jewish doctor in Charleston, and related to my uncle Leo Pearlstine. I've been unable to find evidence to corroborate any of the stories.

Leopold Wetherhorn and Arthur Williams often show up together in Charleston, During the First World War there was a branch of the Jewish Welfare Board in Charleston. In October 1918 the chairman of that organization was Leopold Wetherhorn. Arthur Williams was the Vice Chairman. Both families lived on Wentworth Street. The Wetherhorn family resided at number 123 and the Williams clan lived at 119.

There was one other thing I did find. It was that there was an additional insurance policy on the lumber yard and the insurers refused to pay. The refusal was based on a technical argument. My grandmother sued them. The case was decided in court in Sandusky, OH, in November of 1930. The judge made the insurance company give my grandmother $2000, a fairly large sum in those days. She was also listed as the donor of $1000 to KKBE in 1922. I have a copy of the thank you letter they sent her. After Leopold died Rosa contributed a drinking fountain in his memory. That was in 1928. The thank you letter from the congregation was signed by, guess who, Arthur V. Williams.

My Grandmother, Rosalie Zerline Kahn Wetherhorn, only lived for another 4 years. She died in Charleston on December 25th, 1932. She and her husband are buried in the family plot of the KKBE Huguenin Ave. Cemetery.

Sophie Z Wetherhorn
1898-1971

Spouse	Leo C Pearlstine
Children	Irving M Pearlstine
	Elaine Pearlstine

My personal memory of meeting my aunt, Sophie Pearlstine, right after I was commissioned as a navy ensign, confirmed everything I knew about her. She was an elegant and proper Lady of the Old South. She still had a negro maid whom she could summon using a little button under the edge of the table. I always had that image of her as a proper Lady from a privileged family. Reviewing what I found out about her while preparing this book has not changed that image one bit.

Sophie was the eldest of Leopold and Rosa's children. She was born in Charleston on February 8th, 1898. Here is a picture of her with her father when she was about 2 years old. It is obvious that her father doted on her.

In 1916, when she was just 18 years old, she got her own separate listing in the Charleston City Directory. She was, of course, living at the family home at 123 Wentworth.

The entry also listed her telephone number, 1992J. It was the family number. She did not have her own separate phone. But she did have a separate listing which some of her siblings would also have later on. Her brothers Ernest and Raymond and her uncle Gabriel all got their separate listings in 1918. All three were employed at the family business. Raymond and Ernest were both living at the family home while Gabriel roomed at the YMCA. Her sister, Corinne, received a separate entry in 1919.

Her future husband, Leo Clarence Pearlstine was about 4 years older than Sophie. He had graduated from Clemson University in 1914 with a degree in Civil Engineering. The picture below is from the Clemson 1914 Year book. Notice that he is in cadet corps uniform and his progress through the ranks is listed

Leo volunteered for the army when the USA entered the First World War. He enlisted on May 29th, 1917, received service number 249094382 and was immediately promoted to Corporal, possibly due to his age and education, as already mentioned. In August he was advanced to Sergeant and in September to First Sergeant. Before being sent over- seas in March, 1918, he was made Quartermaster Sergeant Major. In September he was sent to Officer Candidate School, emerging as a Second Lieutenant just before sailing to France in October. His overseas service lasted until April 1919 when he returned to Charleston and he was released from the Army on May 13th, 1919.

After Leo was back in Charleston, he married Sophie. The picture on the previous page shows Sophie in 1921. The young couple went to Cuba for their honeymoon. They returned aboard the SS GENERAL COBB in April, 1920. The passenger manifest lists them as husband and wife and has both of them using the same passport number. However, there was some kind of problem. It's possible that Sophie was simply afraid of sex. The marriage was legally annulled. But Leo persisted. In the end, they were married again in Charleston on October 13th, 1921. This time everything went smoothly. The children, Maynard and Elaine, were born in Charleston in 1922 and 1925.

Mrs. Ruth Jarecky of Dallas, Texas, and Mr. and Mrs. L. Weatherborn of Jacksonville, Fla., were recent visitors of Mr. and Mrs. Leo Pearlstine.

Leo and Sophie were part of the social scene. When my parents and Aunt Ruth Jarecky visited them in 1940 it rated a couple of lines in the local newspaper. The same thing occurred when I was 2 years old. I don't remember the visit, but it was documented in *The Times and Democrat* social column that Leo and Sophie were hosting us when we had been living in Chattanooga.

Sophie died on December 9th, 1971. She was buried in the KKBE Huguenin Street Cemetery in plot South 36 A. Leo died on November 10th, 1980. He was laid to rest alongside her in plot South 36 B

David E Wetherhorn
1899-1968

Spouse   **Philipena B Brown**

Children   David E Wetherhorn

Shirley A Wetherhorn

My Uncle Earnest was born as David Earnest Wetherhorn on February 20th, 1899. But no one ever called him David. He was always Earnest to everyone in the family. This picture shows him as an infant with his parents and older sister, Sophie.

The family business was prospering, and Earnest was given a job within the company. In 1917 he was first listed as a clerk. By 1920 he had been given the title of secretary-treasurer, even though the US census of that year listed him as a salesman. Although he registered for the draft, I found no record of Earnest serving in the First World War. But he did enlist in the South Carolina National Guard. In May 1920 he was a corporal in Company B under the command of Captain William Hawkins when the officers and NCOs went to a 4 day training camp.

In October, 1921, the engagement of Pena Brown, "a most attractive young woman" from Blackville, to Earnest Wetherhorn of Charleston was announced. They were married in Blackville by Rabbi Jacob S. Raisin of KKBE on February 28th, 1922.

Earnest and Pena had their first child, a son, on January 18th, 1923. Their daughter, Shirley Ann, was born on January 24th of the following year. The firstborn was, initially, a happy event. But he quickly developed some kind of problem.

By the time he was 7 he was a resident at the Mattie Gundry Home and School for the Feeble Minded in Falls Church, VA. The family seems to have obliterated him from their collective memory. His sister, my first cousin, apparently did not know he existed. The similarity of this to what the British royal family did to Queen Elizabeth II's cousins, Nerissa and Katherine Bowes-Lyon, was not lost on me. They, too, were confined to an institution and never mentioned, even within the family.

This is the only picture I have ever seen of him. He is still an infant, and is with his father and grandfather.

I don't know when Earnest Jr. was sent to the Gundry Institution. I do know that when I found him there in the 1930 US Census he was almost the youngest person among the 77 individuals that were institutionalized. There were 6 nurses on the staff in addition to a teacher and the owner, Mattie Gundry. Further research into the school yielded more information about the School, but not about Earnest Wetherhorn Jr. Mattie Gundry, whose first name was actually Madeline, was nationally known for her work teaching children with special needs basic knowledge and skills. She opened the Mattie Gundry Home and School for the Feeble Minded in 1899 in Falls Church, VA. It was a pioneering effort to care for individuals who were unable to adjust to "normal" society. The school would later become the Virginia Training School. It was the only school for retarded children in the South and the second largest in the nation. Children were taught occupations including art and rug making, and some were able to support themselves. The good reputation of the school may have influenced the decision to send young Earnest Wetherhorn there.

Earnest and Pena had left the family home to live in their own apartment at 21B St Philip St. After the Wetherhorn lumber yard was destroyed by fire Earnest continued to work in the same profession, but now he was a salesman for S. M. Parker Lumber. He and Pena moved back in to his parents' home at 123 Wentworth temporarily. They later moved to Halsey St., and after that made their home at 16 Pitt.

By 1934 Earnest was the sales manager for Parker and the family returned, once again, to 123 Wentworth.

By the time the period covered in this story ended they were renting apartment 10 at 135 Wentworth and he was working for General Woodworking Co. at 5 Pinckney Street.

After retiring, Earnest and Pena moved into a retirement home. He died in Charleston in June 1968 and Pena followed him in July 1973.

Daughter, Shirley Ann, married Frank Jacob Glaser. Together they raised 3 sons and a daughter in Virginia Beach, VA. He died on January 6th, 2001 and she on September 9th 2012. They were a U S Air Force family.

Raymond Wetherhorn
1900-1948

Spouse	**Mary Lucille Moore**
Spouse	**Rosalie Pauline May**
Children	Mitchell H Wetherhorn
	Norma M Wetherhorn

My Uncle Raymond was born in Charleston on July 25th, 1900. The only picture I have of him is taken from a family photo dated around 1920.

He was just 17 when he was first listed in the city directory. At that time he was recorded as the assistant manager of the family lumber yard. That year was when the United States went to war against Germany. Raymond was taken into the Army assigned serial number 814066 and trained to be a soldier. He was assigned as a private to B Company of the 604th Engineer Battalion. His unit was sent to France on the British liner SS CARMANIA on September First, 1918. The armistice came on November 11th; just over 2 months after Raymond reached France. As a late arrival, he had to wait to return home. On June 10th, 1919, his unit embarked on the navy battleship USS NEW HAMPSHIRE in Brest, France. The NEW HAMPSHIRE, like many other large navy warships, was employed bringing the soldiers of the American Expeditionary Force back to the USA. The NEW HAMPSHIRE made four trips across the Atlantic doing this. She carried about 1260 returning soldiers when the 604th Engineers came home. One of the soldiers died on board before the ship docked in Newport News on

Sunday, June 22nd. The soldiers slept in hammocks. There were movies every day. And in spite of the season, there was enough of a swell to make many of the army passengers sea sick.

Raymond returned to work in the family business. On October 28th, 1922 he married Rosalie Pauline May, whom everyone called Rollie. Rollie had been a student at the College of Charleston after graduating from Menninger High School in 1918. The photo of Rollie, the only one I currently have, was cropped from a 1973 High School reunion.

Their son, Mitchell Harris, was born on August 21st, 1923. He was followed by a daughter, Norma May, on October 18th, 1925. The children were still infants when tragedy struck the family.

First, the Wetherhorn lumber yard burned down. That left Raymond, as well as others, without employment. When his father died the following year Raymond was very likely under intense personal pressure. He had a wife and 2 small children to support. I suspect it was too much of a burden. My cousin Maynard told me that sometime in 1928 Raymond just disappeared. Rollie took the children to live with her mother and sister in Richmond, VA. She filed for divorce in Florida in 1930 citing the cause as "abandonment". Someone, possibly the court clerk, changed that to "desertion". The divorce was granted.

Rollie and her sister, who was also divorced, remained in Florida. The children grew up there. Mitchell became a psychologist after serving in the US Army in WWII. He married an English girl and took her back to America. They settled in Alaska. Norma married a dentist and raised her family in Florida.

I eventually found a clue that helped me find out about Raymond. There was a cryptic entry in a local newspaper in Kalispell, Montana saying "Raymond Wetherhorn of Essex was in town yesterday on business". Looking for items in the Pacific Northwest helped me to find Portland Oregon city directories showing him living in that city. In 1937 and 1938 he was listed at 2114 South West 1st, apt 25, in Portland. Another local newspaper article indicated he was employed as a timekeeper at Commercial Iron Works. He listed them as his employer when he registered for the draft in 1942. The registration report gave his height as 5'7", and his weight as 190 pounds.

After the war was over, in early 1946, Raymond married Mary Lucille Moore in Portland. He died on Adak Island, Alaska, on October 1st 1948. His body was cremated and the urn with his ashes placed in the Portland Oregon, River View Cemetery, Main Mausoleum, Corridor 1, Niche 504.

Rollie died in Miami, Florida on August 11th, 1985 after living in Miami for half a century.

Corinne M Wetherhorn 1902-1985

Spouse   **Herman Pickus**

Children   Leone W Pickus

               Herman M Pickus Jr

Corinne Marcelle Wetherhorn was born in Charleston on June 2oth, 1902. When she was a child she had a love of pickles. Her siblings responded to this by calling her "pickles". The nickname stayed with her in many family conversations for the rest of her life.

The American Israelite newspaper carried a story on page 1 listing the confirmation classes in various congregations around the country. Corinne was one of 8 members of the KKBE confirmation class led by Rabbi Jacob Raisin.

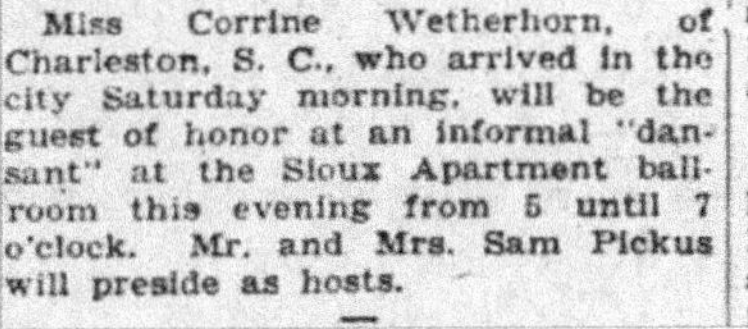

Miss Corrine Wetherhorn, of Charleston, S. C., who arrived in the city Saturday morning, will be the guest of honor at an informal "dansant" at the Sioux Apartment ballroom this evening from 5 until 7 o'clock. Mr. and Mrs. Sam Pickus will preside as hosts.

I don't know how or when Corinne met her future husband, Herman Pickus. The first clue I have to their romance is a clipping from the *Sioux City Journal* society page Sunday, December 6th, 1925

The 1922 Charleston City Directory gave her a separate line entry. Her younger sisters, Mildred and Rosalie also were given separate entries. But all of them were shown as living at the family home at 123 Wentworth, and with the same telephone number, 3108.

Sam Pickus was Herman's older brother. Of course, Sioux City is a long way from Charleston. What happened to bring Corrine to Sioux City? I don't know. What I do know is that the Iowa state census of 1925 had Herman living at the home of Bertha and Mike Sakalovsky in Woodbury, Iowa. Bertha was Herman's oldest sister. Another Pickus sister, Esther, was married to another Sakalovsky brother, Morris. However they met, Corrine and Herman were married in 1927. They sailed to Havana, Cuba, for their honeymoon and returned to NY aboard the passenger liner ORIZABA at the end of February, 1927. From there they went to Aberdeen, South Dakota, where Herman started his road construction business.

Before proceeding further I want to go back in order to mention a few more facts about Herman. He was about 5' 7" tall and weighed 180 pounds in 1918. I did not find a service record, but I believe he served in the Army in World War One. At that time he still had dark hair to match his brown eyes. But his hair became thinner and thinner and he was soon quite bald. The lack of hair was sufficient to expose a small scar on the top of his head.

Corinne and Herman initially lived at 1002 S Washington in Aberdeen and Herman's business, The Aberdeen Construction Company, later the H. Pickus Construction Co., had an office at 117 ½ S. Main. That was their home when daughter Leone Wetherhorn Pickus was born on April 2nd 1928 and also when son Herman Mayer Pickus Junior was born on January 18th, 1930.

Herman's construction business was involved mostly in selling gravel and building roads and culverts within Brown County. It was a profitable arrangement that left the family able to engage a young girl to help in the house for about 4 months in 1930. She was paid about $50 a month. The young lady then got married and no longer worked for them. My father was unemployed around that time and Herman hired him to work in road and bridge construction projects. This would ultimately lead to my parents meeting one another. That story properly belongs in another chapter.

Despite a legal battle with state and county officials that dragged on for some time the road construction business was still profitable. Corinne and Herman were able to take a vacation in Mexico with his brother, Sam, and Sam's wife Ida. They even sent my parents a postcard from Mexico with their picture on it.

This takes their chapter past the 1940 cut-off date, Herman died in Aberdeen on November 1st, 1971. Corinne died there on October 1st, 1985. My cousin Maynard told me she died from congestive heart failure, Corinne and Herman rest alongside each other in Mount Sinai Cemetery in Sioux City, Iowa.

Leone married Dr. Jack Paradise in 1947, They divorced in 1968, Herman Jr. whom we all called "Brother" or "Buddy", stayed in Aberdeen. One of his grandchildren was named Corinne after her great grandmother. Herman Jr. died in Aberdeen on January 6th, 2012.

Rosalie A Wetherhorn
1904-1969

Spouse	**Lewis Bear Rosenau**
Children	Lewis Bear Rosenau Jr
	Richard E Rosenau

Popular Bride

Rosalie Wetherhorn was born in Charleston on February 27th, 1904. Her family nickname was "Rusty". I never found out how she got it.

I also don't know how she met Lewis Baer Rosenau from Pensacola, FL. During World War One he had sailed as a mariner for the US Shipping Board. His travels might have taken him to Charleston. In any case, at some point they did meet. After the war he came to Charleston to see her. After one of those visits their engagement was announced. He was about 5 years older than she. The actual wedding took place at the Wetherhorn home in Charleston on August 1st, 1928 and was followed by a large reception. The couple then set off to make their way in the world.

Lewis landed a job as manager of The Parisian in Mobile Alabama. It was a branch of a local chain of department stores in that state, selling housewares, clothing, footwear, jewelry, furniture, bedding, and beauty products. Rosalie worked as the assistant manager of the same store. Mobile is about 533 miles West of Pensacola. Today it takes around an hour to make the drive. Then in took a bit longer. They lived in Mobile until at least 1931. When they moved back to Pensacola Lewis opened a women's wear store named The Fashion Shop at 105 S. Palafox. His younger brother, Sam, had an insurance agency just down the street at 228 S. Palafox. Lewis and Rosalie stayed at the San Carlos Hotel. The 7 story hotel was located at the center of Pensacola. Palafox divided the city streets between East and West. The Hotel was at the corner of Garden Street which marked the division between North and South. It was an architectural landmark until it was destroyed in 1997.

Lewis and Rosalie later moved to share a home with Lewis's widowed mother at 312 N. Spring St. Meanwhile, Rosalie became vice president of a chain store company named Milrose Hat Stores. Lewis gave up on clothing and went to work at selling wholesale liquor, where he expected to make a better living. In 1936 their first son, Lewis Junior, was born. A second son, Richard, followed in 1939 The following picture shows them all a few years later.

Lewis Rosenau moved up in the liquor business to become the sales manager for Standard Distributing Company. It was a good enough job for them to own their home at 1831 Blount Ave. He died on April 25th, 1959 and was buried in the Temple Beth El Cemetery in Pensacola. Rosalie survived until December 15th, 1969. She was laid to rest alongside her husband.

Their sons seem to have a hard time managing relationships, Lewis Jr. was married 8 times, and Richard, who was known as "Dickie", was married 4 times. Lewis Jr. was working and in Tallahassee when he died in 1988. He was also buried in the Pensacola Temple Beth El Cemetery. When this was being written Richard was still alive in Florida.

Mildred Wetherhorn
1905-1978

Spouse	**Henry Aloysius Love**
Spouse	**Abraham E Gandler**
Children	Leonard M Gandler

Mildred Wetherhorn was born in Charleston on Thursday, May 25th, 1905. Half way around the world the Imperial Russian Second Pacific Squadron was steaming towards Vladivostok. Two days later it would nearly be annihilated by the Japanese near Tsushima in one of the most one-sided naval battles the world ever saw. Millie, as she was known to most, grew up as the daughter of a well-known and respected member of the Charleston community. When she was 16 she even got her own listing in the city directory.

Things changed when the family owned lumber yard burned down. Her father died shortly thereafter and the family was no longer among the wealthy. By 1928 Millie had taken a job as a stenographer at the Southern Printing and Publishing Company. The company offices were in their own building located at 125 Meeting Street. Meanwhile, her mother sold part of the family home to Mr. Bernard O'Neill. He owned and operated the Central Service Station and the attached Central Auto Laundry. The O'Neill part of the house was designated 123a Wentworth. The Wetherhorn part was called 123b.

Somewhere along the way Millie met Abraham Edward Gandler from Cincinnati. A romance blossomed, and they were married on April 1st, 1929. The couple was living in Richmond, VA at 3132 Park Ave, apartment 2, in 1930. But the April 10th US Census that year caught Millie visiting in Charleston with her mother and younger brother, Leo, at the home of her sister Sophie. Edward Gandler started out working as a salesman, but in 1933 he had moved up to be the manager of the Lenard's store in Montgomery, AL. The Gandlers later moved to Mobile, AL. Edward was employed as the manager at Boyd's Inc., a store that handled mostly women's clothing. Their only child, Leonard, was born in Charleston on June 1st, 1930.

Edward died in Mobile on May 18th, 1950. He was buried in Ahavat Chesed Cemetery. Leonard joined the US Air Force. I re- member him when he was briefly stationed at Lowry AFB in Den- ver. He operated a plant for making oxygen for pilots and aircrew. Millie came to see him. It was the last time I saw either of them. I remember going with Leonard to get the brakes fixed on his old second hand car. He had attached a rope to the hand brake and pulled on it whenever he needed to stop or slow. When I told my parents about the adventure they were quite upset with both of us for taking such a risk.

Millie remarried in May 1956. This lasted only a year. She divorced Henry A. Love in 1957. Millie died on September 28th, 1978, in Mobile and was buried under the name Mildred W. Gandler in the Springhill Avenue Temple Cemetery.

When stationed at Fairchild Air Force Base Leonard married Elvira B. Foote. She had been married and divorced three times before. The marriage was performed by a justice of the peace in her home town of Coeur D'Alene Idaho on February 3rd 1964. Leonard left the Air Force as a staff sergeant the following year, after 15 years of service. He never had children and I do not know what ever became of his wife. Leonard died January 17th, 1980 in Mobile and is buried near his mother.

Leopold Wetherhorn Jr
1908-1987

Spouse	Hilma E Kahn
Children	Sally Wetherhorn

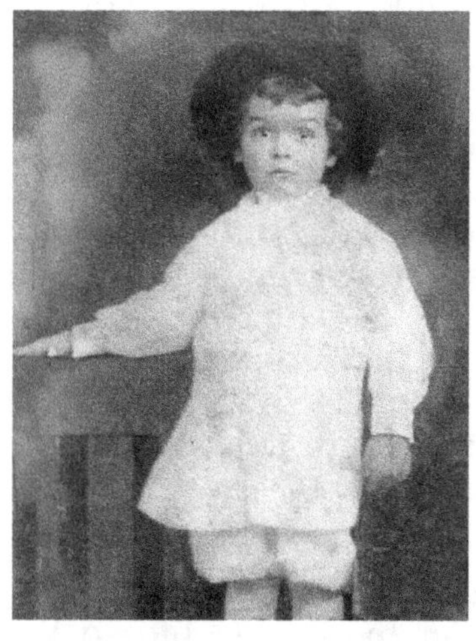

Leopold Wetherhorn Jr, always known in the family as Leo, was born in Charleston on October 9th, 1908. The photo here was taken about 1910.

Leo was always interested in athletics. He was 5'10 ½" tall and weighed 179 pounds. In High School he was the fullback for the school team. After high school he found employment as an electrician at the Charleston Navy Yard.

This next photo of Leo on p. 135 was taken in 1935.

In 1934 The Pensacola newspaper carried the announcement of the engagement of Leo Wetherhorn to Hilma Kahn. Hilma was a first cousin of Lewis Bear Rosenau, the husband of Leo's sister, Rosalie. The marriage took place in Pensacola on May 19th, 1935. Leo rented a home at 158 Pitt in Charleston for $40 a month.

Leo resumed his job as a 40 hours a week electrician at the Navy Yard. In 1930 he continued to live at the family home at 123 Wentworth with his mother and sister, Millie. He did so even though the house was officially listed as owned by his brother-in-law, Leo Pearlstine. Of course, Sophie and Leo and their 2 children also lived there.

Their daughter, Sally, was born on September 6th, 1940. She still lives in Charleston. Leo died on October 26th, 1987. Hilma survived until December 9th, 2001. They are buried, side by side, in the Wetherhorn section of the KKBE Huguenin Avenue Cemetery in plots South 42 A and B.

Levy L Wetherhorn
1912-1983

Spouse	**Gertrude Weisman**
Children	Lee M Wetherhorn
	Randi K Wetherhorn

Levy Lester Wetherhorn was born in Charleston on New Year's Day 1912. He was named Levy in honor of his grandfather who had passed away nearly 2 years earlier. He almost never used that name. He was listed as L. Lester Wetherhorn in many documents. He went by the name Lester, or Les, most of his life. But inside the family his siblings all called him "Duke". When queried why he got that nickname he always said they called him Duke because he was no Count. Here he is as a toddler, on the left, with his older brother, Leo.

Les was always a great sports fan. He loved athletics, both as a participant and as an observer. He was a lifelong bowler, and played in local leagues wherever he lived. He engaged in amateur boxing, and after he was married he actually played semi-professional baseball for the team from Sears, Roebuck, and Co., where he worked. Playing baseball actually put an end to his sports career. He broke his ankle sliding into a base during a game. That put him permanently off participation in most competitive sports. The following clippings all mention him during different phases of his sports career,

WILDCATS DEFEAT TYPHOONS, 25-12

WEST PALM BEACH. Nov. 15. Miami Beach's hardluck Typhoons suffered their fourth setback of the season Friday night as the West Palm Beach Wildcats turned breaks into touchdowns for a 25-12 victory.

MIAMI BEACH	Pos.	W. P. BEACH
Brumlick	LE	R. Widell
Resnick	LT	R. Widell
Tesney	LG	Brady
Bronner	C	Thompson
Banakon	RG	Whidden
Schwartz	RT	Lance
Weatherhorn	RE	O'Neal
Kunde	QT	Riggs
Meyer	LH	Obee
Manson	RH	Mauro
Cooper	FB	Clark

American football

Anhorn Takes Weatherhorn

Vic Anhorn of Lake Preston, a Huron college freshman, found himself in plenty of trouble early in his bout with Les Wetherhorn of Huron, being unable to cope with the two fisted attack of the local light heavyweight. After being pushed about the ring in the opening chapter the collegian forced Wetherhorn into retreat in the second round as he pummelled him severely. Wetherhorn made a strong last round bid but could not keep out of Anhorn's range and the bout was stopped, the Lake Preston boxer winning by a technical knockout.

Boxing

ST. JOSEPH TEAM WINS

B'nai B'rith Tourney Goes to Polsky on 3,091

Polsky Motors of St. Joseph clicked for 3,091 to claim the team championship in the Kansas City B'nai B'rith handicap bowling tournament at King Louie East lanes. Circle Auto Parts trailed with 3,033.

Les Wetherhorn nudged Henry Dloogoff, 716-686, for the singles crown. Sal Daniels and Max Tonkin combined for 1,271 in doubles, 5 pins better than Mickey Lewin and Josh Markowitz. Al Clayman and Marvin Nelson finished 1-2 in all-events with 1,896 and 1,877. Wetherhorn's 652 and 266s by Wolf Cohen and Sal Daniels were high scratch scores.

bowling

He continued to bowl for many years and was one of the better bowlers in the Bnai Brith Leagues in Denver and in Kansas City.

But that's getting a bit ahead of the story. My grandfather died when Les was still in High school. He was a good student, and proficient enough to be appointed as a Lab Assistant in Chemistry. That job meant he had keys to the Chemistry Lab storeroom. It was an opportunity he just couldn't let pass. One day, when things seemed quiet, he used the keys to open the storeroom. He took out a small piece of metallic sodium and locked the door. Metallic Sodium can be dangerous. It reacts with water. That's why it was always stored in a jar of oil. Les took an old glass milk bottle and filled it part way with water. He put it on the window ledge. Then he dumped the metallic sodium into the bottle, slammed a cork into the top to seal it, and hightailed it out of the room. The metal didn't last long on the sunlit ledge. There was a big bang and broken glass scattered all over. Sadly, my father was found out. He wasn't expelled, but he lost the Lab assistant job.

I knew this story when I went off to the University of Michigan some years later. I lived in a dormitory with several two person rooms on the upstairs corridor. There was one three person room in the middle. The occupants of that room were always boisterous and took great joy in disturbing the rest of their neighbors. I conspired with my roommate to teach them a lesson in humility. I went to their room and pretended to have a question that they might be able to help answer. I positioned myself on the window sill so that they would be looking at me, and not at the door to the room. Meanwhile, my roommate made a neat pile of a mixture of sulfur and powdered aluminum just inside the door. For those of you who don't know, that's a simple formula for early photographic flash powder. When he was finished, I thanked the guys in the room for their help and left, closing the door behind me. Once outside the room, we squirted some liquid cigarette lighter fluid under the door, and lit it. We quickly retired to our room. There was a loud POUF. Their room, and the entire hallway, was filled with smoke. The bottom of the door was scorched. The end result was that the room occupants had to pay for replacing the door, and they were put on probation. The real culprits, my roommate and I, were never discovered.

Much later, when I was married and had a family, this story remained a secret until our children were old enough to be able to keep it from their children. Now the cat's out of the bag.

It's time to go back to my father's story. He was actually initially expected to attend Columbia University. He even moved to New York to live with his Aunt, Hannah Link. That's when fate, in the form of the Great Depression, stepped in.

Money was tight. Les left school and moved to Aberdeen, South Dakota where he had work with his brother-in-law, Herman Pickus. Herman's construction firm had contracts for building roads and bridges inside the state. My Dad was dating a nice young woman named Rose Weisman. She had to leave Aberdeen for a while and asked her sister, Gertrude, to fill in for her while she was away. That's how my parents met. This is Les around 1935.

Gertrude was one of 8 children whose parents had fled Russia in 1905. They left after the horrible Kishinev Pogrom of 1903 and before the failed 1905 Russian Revolution. Gertrude's father got a homestead grant in McIntosh County, North Dakota. The terms were that the homesteader had to live on the land,

and make improvements (building a house there was considered as having done that) and at the end of ten years the land was his, free and clear. Gertrude was born on the farm. When her father sold the farm and used the money to open a little store, she even helped out. The store was in McLaughlin, South Dakota, on the edge of the Standing Rock Sioux Indian Reservation. She learned to count in Lakota, the Sioux language, in order to make change. I learned to count to ten in Lakota from her. My children learned it from me. But that's probably where it will stop. I didn't expect to hear my grandchildren counting

"Wahnjee, Nopa, Yaminee, Topa" while playing hide and seek in Israel. Here is my mother and her younger brother, William, whom everyone called Buddy, in front of the town drugstore and soda fountain in McLaughlin around 1927.

My Mother, and her sister, Valva Weisman, were just a year apart in age. In high school they were in the same class. If a teacher called on one of them and she hesitated with an answer, the other would step in to answer. They did not dress alike. Both went to Northern State Teacher's College, where they tried the same maneuver. But the professors soon caught on. They would ask for an answer from "Miss Weisman in the blue dress." At one time there were 4 Weisman sisters at the college at the same time.

traveling public.

Four Sisters Taking Courses At Northern

ABERDEEN, Feb. 3—Northern State Teachers college at Aberdeen boasts of four sisters on its enrollment list. Rose, Jennie, Valva and Gertrude Weisman of McLaughlin are all attending the Aberdeen school. Miss Rose Weisman is taking work in night school in the Commercial department, Miss Jennie Weisman is taking extension work in the history department and Miss Valva and Gertrude Weisman are enrolled as regular students.

Gertrude Weisman

Aberdeen, Nov. 14—Miss Gertrude Weisman, McLaughlin, has been selected editor-in-chief of the Pasque, yearbook at Northern normal.

Gert was appointed the editor in chief of the school yearbook, *The Pasque*, in 1931. The book appeared in 1933 and was heralded as one of the best ever produced.

Gertrude and Valva Weisman later transferred to the University of Minnesota to complete their degrees.

My mother was also accepted into the Jewish sorority Sigma Delta Tau that promotes academic achievement and empowering women.

Here are Valva and Gertrude graduating in 1934. Valva is on the left.

Mom had a couple of jobs teaching high school home economics in rural North Dakota. She was all of 5 feet 2 inches tall. She told me she was once assigned to supervise a study hall period where the students had a break from regular classes. The floor of the room was covered with little wads of paper called spitballs. The students used to waft them at one another for "sport". Mom caught one of them, a 6 foot plus football star, in the

Sigma Delta Tau, in recent ceremonies, initiated Miss Bertha Millunchick of St. Paul, Miss Gertrude Weisman of McIntosh, S. D., and Miss Lillian Millman of Sioux

act. As she was approaching him he let fly his last spitball, aimed at another student. It hit my mother instead of his intended target. She walked up to him and reached up and slapped his face. She then commanded him to get down on the floor and pick up one hundred of the spitballs. He was obviously shocked that this diminutive teacher would do such a thing to him. He promptly went to his knees and did precisely what she had told him.

Being a teacher meant she had free time in the summer and was therefore able to step in to help her older sister, Rose. That brings us back to Aberdeen. Mom and Dad quickly became an "item". Les proposed, Gert accepted, and a wedding was scheduled for spring, 1938. But when the scheduled date was just around the corner, the Rabbi called to say he was called away for a funeral and would not be able to officiate on that day. My mother quickly got on the telephone and called another Rabbi in Minneapolis. Yes, he would be free and happy to officiate,

"And what is the groom's name, Miss Weisman?" he asked.

"Lester Wetherhorn," she replied.

"I'm Sorry, Miss Weisman," said the Rabbi, somewhat indignantly, "I do not perform mixed marriages."

"I'm Sorry, too, Rabbi, "she replied, "But Mr. Wetherhorn IS Jewish."

The Rabbi asked for a reference, which was duly given, and the wedding proceeded as planned.

Here is a photo of my mother's family taken at the wedding on June 23rd, 1938. My parents are in the center, flanked by my mother's parents. In the front row are my older cousins from Mom's side. The back row is all her siblings, including the spouses of the two who were already married.

My parents settled in Jacksonville, Florida. Dad worked as a salesman for Sears Roebuck. He played baseball on the company team and was a junior salesman in the men's wear department. That's where this next story came from.

A possible customer came in. He was wearing dirty clothes and looked quite unkempt. The senior salesmen were unwilling to help him. They worked, in part, on a commission basis. This man didn't look like he would spend much. They passed him down the line to the junior salesman. Dad approached him and asked if he could help. The man selected a lot of items, suit, shirts, tie, etc. And when it finally came time to pay he reached into a torn pocket and came out with a roll of bills that was as big as his fist. He peeled off several of them to pay for his purchases and left. Dad always told me that this just shows you should not pre-judge anyone by his outward appearance.

I was born on January 8th, 1940. I had some birthmarks that were considered potentially dangerous in those days. We went to Minneapolis to have them removed by a relatively new process called radiation, using Radium. Then we returned to Jacksonville. That's where we were when the Japanese attacked Pearl Harbor. Dad went to the local shipyard to see if he could find work to support the war effort. The man who interviewed him asked if he could read a blueprint. He said he thought he could. The interviewer rolled out a real blueprint on the table and asked what a certain symbol meant. Dad told him. He asked about another one and again got an immediate, and accurate, response. At that point, the way Dad described it; he sat back in his chair, pushed his hat back on his head, and exclaimed "I'll be damned. You CAN read a blueprint".

Les worked in the Jacksonville shipyard building Liberty Ships for the next 3 years. He was the leading man in charge of a 3 person team erecting boiler flats inside the new ships. When the Battle of the Atlantic was won he lost his occupational deferment and was reclassified by the draft board as being available for military service. He didn't want to be called up to join the army and leave us (Mom and me) in Jacksonville, so we moved to Denver. My aunt Ann, Mom's sister, had a large house with enough room for us to also move in. After we did, Dad got a job in an ammunition plant and ended up having his essential occupation deferment renewed.

I've already strayed past the 1940 end of stories limit. Dad died in Denver on May 3rd, 1983. Mom died on August 15th, 2001, in Florida, where she had gone to be near my sister. They are both buried, side by side, in the Denver Jewish Cemetery.

Jenette Wetherhorn
1875-1962

Spouse	**Louis J Flanders**
Children	Hannah Flanders
	Sadie Flanders p. 147

Jenette Wetherhorn was born in Charleston on April 26th 1875. She attended religious school at KKBE congregation where the rabbi, David Levy, taught and supervised a staff of a principal and 12 other teachers. The 1890 confirmation class was honored with a graduation event held in the temple on Sunday, May 25th. Honoring the confirmation class in this manner had not been done for several years. The rabbi spoke while all the confirmation class sat on the stage. The report in *The American Israelite* carried the text of his speech, and noted how beautifully the temple had been decorated "in nature's own garb" by members of the Happy Workers Society.

Jenette, known to the family as Nettie, was joined in the class by her younger brother, Marcus and 13 other young men and women. All the class, and the staff, then went to Rabbi Levy's home for a reception.

The Sumter SC local paper, *The Watchman and Southron*, reported on a major social event in the June 24th edition. The event was the annual "Distribution Hop". For those readers who are younger, a Hop was a term used for a formal or semi-formal dance. The paper called it "The most enjoyable and largest attended dance of the year, a fit ending for Sumter's society season". The Wetherhorn family was well represented by Nettie, who was just 16, and her brother Leo (Leopold), then 19, and cousin Julius, aged 20. Also among the guests were Rosa Kahn, 18, Leopold's future bride, and her sister Fannie.

When she was 25 Nettie was married in Charleston to Louis Flanders on November 27th, 1898. Her husband was 12 years older than she. Reverend Barnett Elzas officiated. Elzas had replaced Rabbi Levy at the helm of KKBE in 1894.

The newly wedded couple established their home in New York City at 177 East 77th. Louis' brother Jack lived with them, and they had a black servant girl named Hatty. Their first daughter, Hannah was born on October 9th, 1900, while they were still at that address. Louis worked as a salesman in men's clothing.

The Flanders' second daughter, Sadie, was born 2 years later. She has her own chapter later. The family moved around from place to place. In 1910 they were living at 120 West 139th. At that time Nettie's younger brothers, Mitchell and Henry, were with them. Louis was officially listed as the manager of a haberdashery. That's just a fancy word for a store dealing in men's clothing and accessories. They still had a servant; in 1910 it was Marian Batson from the British West Indies.

Having 2 daughters apparently made keeping a servant an expense they could not maintain. They also had wedding expenses. The girls had been stenographers after high school, but then they married. Hannah was wed to Donald A. Finberg on February 9th, 1922. The Flanders' West side homes were also probably cheaper than the original East side apartment. In any case the next home was on Fort Washington Ave. where the rent was $80 per month. Hannah soon divorced Donald Finberg and came back to live with her parents. They had no children. Also, after the divorce, she began using the name Helen or Helene Flanders.

When Charles Lindbergh made his historic solo flight across the Atlantic in May, 1927, the news reached Louis and Nettie, along with the rest of the world, via 2 forms of media. There was radio coverage from Le Bourget airfield in Paris. Live broadcasts also accompanied Lindbergh's arrival home in NY and in Washington, DC. The Flanders family owned a radio receiver at that time. There was also extensive coverage in the newspapers. The *New York Times*, among others, put the story on their front page. Many smaller newspapers ran an identical story that they received from the Associated Press. AP provided this kind of coverage for newspapers that could not afford to have their own correspondents on the scene when big stories broke anywhere in the world. AP was actually formed in 1846 and got a major boost with the establishment of telegraph communication. A similar front page syndicated story was in dozens of papers in 1932 when baby Charles Lindbergh Jr was kidnapped and killed in 1932.

As Louis grew older he began a slow drop down the ladder of responsibility. He returned to being a salesman, and later was employed as a shipping clerk. Hannah/Helene worked as a secretary for a chemical manufacturing plant. Louis Flanders died on February 26th, 1946. His wife survived him by several years. Nettie died on October 11th 1962.

Sadie Flanders
1902-1977

Spouse   **Alfred Edward Boas**

Children   Melvin Gabriel Boas

                    Richard Stuart Boas

Sadie Flanders was born in New York on April 1st, 1902. Everyone knew her as Peggy. In 1920 the Flanders family lived at 14 W. 144th, just down the street from the main branch of the New York Public Library. That building had only opened to the public on May 23rd, 1911 after being under construction for nearly 16 years and costing about $9 million.

The site of Grand Central Terminal is also very near. The terminal, the world's largest, had opened on February 1st, 1913, and joined railroad commuter links to the IRT (Interurban Rapid Transit) subway line that had opened in 1904.

Peggy had worked as a stenographer after high school. Then she met Alfred Edward Boas. They were married on June 17th, 1923. Alfred Boas was named Abraham Boas on his Passport and in his WWI service record. His father had died when he was still a toddler and he had been living with his widowed mother and three brothers. When the US entered World War One Abraham/Alfred enlisted in the Navy on May 4th 1917. His older brother was already married and was not drafted while his youngest brother was still too young to be accepted in the army. His younger brother, Benjamin, also enlisted in the Navy on November 15th, 1917. Alfred was only 5' 4 ½" tall, a good 2 inches shorter than his brothers. He found himself assigned to headquarters of the 3d Naval District in NY. He worked in the office and with the training unit that was established at Columbia University. Alfred and Benjamin were both advanced to the rating of Chief Yeoman before they were released from active service at the end of the war. They also both needed glasses.

Alfred found employment with an import-export firm dealing primarily with Latin America. His work took him to Havana, Cuba and to Rio de Janeiro and possibly also to

Panama, Jamaica, and Puerto Rico. The company he represented, the Flexite Corporation, apparently dealt with silicone based chemical products and included a special Flexite airless automobile tire. The following photograph, from his 1919 passport application, shows his neat moustache, but not his glasses.

Peggy was a housewife, a position that was probably held in higher esteem at that time. The family name sometimes appears as Boaz and sometimes as Boas. They had two sons. Melvin was born on April 9th, 1924. His brother, Richard, was born on May 7th, 1927. Most of Richard's life is outside the date range of this history. Melvin, however, has a story that just finishes outside that range. When Japan attacked Pearl Harbor Melvin was not yet 18 years old. He followed his father's example and enlisted in the Air Corps on November 24th, 1942. He was also physically close to his father, being 5' 3" tall and weighing only 125 pounds. Melvin was given serial number 12188896, did his basic training and was sent to an airbase in England. On March 14th, 1944, he was the victim of a freak accident. The hospital admission record says he died of a cerebral hemorrhage caused by a rifle bullet, not a result of enemy action. It was defined as a non-battle injury sustained in the line of duty. The senior European Theater Jewish Chaplain, CAPT Judah Nadich, was in touch with the local Jewish Welfare Board and the JWB record card indicates three additional follow up contacts. I never found additional details about his tragic death.

After retiring, Peggy and Alfred moved to Florida. Peggy died there on July 6th, 1977.Alfred died in Florida on September 20th, 1983.

Gabriel   Wetherhorn
1877-1924

Henry   Wetherhorn
1879-1922

Spouse   Angela Fitzgerald

Mitchell   Wetherhorn
1881-1914

Spouse   Emma Mullowney

Gabriel Wetherhorn was born in Charleston on December 3rd, 1877. His Brother Henry was born on September 18th 1979. Their brother Mitchell was born on April 6th, 1881. None had children. I put them together because their parents section was already quite long and also because their lives were intertwined.

It looks to me as if Levy Wetherhorn made a real effort to provide for his children. He had married off the girls, and set his oldest son, Leopold, to take over the lumber yard business. Gabriel started out as clerk for J.L. David and son in 1901. Not long after that was given a job in the family firm, too. By 1910 he was the company bookkeeper. He left the family business, got his own home in Charleston at 74 Society, and became a traveling salesman for the Loose-Wiles Biscuit Company.

The two youngest brothers, Henry and Mitchell, attended the College of Charleston. Then they went to New York and attended Columbia University. Henry graduated from Columbia with a Law degree while Mitchell was still at College of Charleston. Their older sister, Hannah, had moved to NY before her husband died. Her home became their residence, a home away from home. Henry tried to become better known in NY by helping organize an association of former SC residents called "Sons of the Palmetto State" in 1906. He was the first treasurer of the group. Initially, Henry opened a law firm, Wetherhorn and Link, even though his brother-in-law apparently was not an official lawyer. The office was located in room 804 at 160 Nassau. In 1910 their office was located in room 504 at 146 Broadway. They managed to earn a living by handling real estate transactions. At that time the entire clan was living at 2453 7th Avenue. That included Gabriel, who had come to NY representing the family lumber business. Both Henry and Mitchell were officially admitted to the bar in NY. They appear in the listing of new lawyers issued on January 30th, 1913. The law firm office was now listed as Wetherhorn and Wetherhorn.

Mitchell married Emma Mullowney on October 26th, 1911. It's likely that she had been one of their secretaries. Mitchell and Henry decided to try their luck in California. They moved to Pasadena and opened an office in room 502 at 116 Temple in Pasadena. They were admitted to the California bar based on their NY licenses. Mitchell was not well. He returned to Charleston and died of tuberculosis there on June 23rd, 1914.

Henry married Angela Fitzgerald Lambert in California on February 2nd, 1917. Another genealogist reported that they divorced a year later, but he gave no source, and I was never able to confirm the divorce. Angela did remarry, to automobile service station owner Herbert Charles Scherer. But that only happened much later.

Henry won a serious breach of contract suit, V. C. Emden vs Harry Hoffler, for $12,286.16. This was reported in the *San Francisco Recorder* on July 19th, 1920. That case may have been what got him started. As a part of Wetherhorn, Hoyt, and Jones he represented Seena Owen, one of the biggest silent film stars of the time. She was being paid $1500 a week in 1920. She was involved in a three way suit with two other top stars, George Walsh, her husband, and Estelle Taylor, one of the prettiest starlets in the city. The end result was a divorce for the married couple and loads of grist for the gossip columnists of the day. As part of Wetherhorn and Scarborough he also represented William S. Hart, another top star of the silent film era Westerns. Hart was nicknamed Two Gun Bill and had a solid acting reputation from his earlier career acting on stage. He later took up writing and directing.

Henry was unable to enjoy much of the notoriety that followed. He died on July 30th, 1922.

Gabriel had remained in NY and died in the Bronx on January 12th, 1924 at the age of 46.

Hermine Wetherhorn
1883-1979

Spouse	**Irving W Schwarz**
Children	Louis Schwarz

Hermine Wetherhorn, known as Mina, was born on December 21st, 1883, in Charleston. She was the youngest of Levy and Pena's children. Mina was one of nine children to complete Rabbi Elzas's confirmation class of 1898 at Temple Beth Elohim in May of that year.

Mina traveled to visit her cousins in Georgia in 1903. That got her a mention in the *Savannah Daily News* society column as an attendee at the YMHA costume party with her cousin Sophie.

As a young woman of 22 she went to visit her cousin, Pauline Jarecky, in St. Matthews. The two were less than a year apart in age. Pauline staged an "At Home" party for Mina that rated a detailed report in the local paper.

The 'Miss Hennie' mentioned in the paper is Henrietta Jarecky, Pauline's younger sister.

Two years later, on June 2nd, 1907 Mina married Irving Schwartz. Rabbi Elzas may have officiated. Elzas left Charleston in 1910 and in 1917 published a book of Jewish marriage notices from Charleston. His book covers marriages only up to the end of 1906, prior to Mina's wedding.

An At Home.

At St. Matthews on Tuesday afternoon of last week from 4.30 to 7.30 o'clock Miss Pauline Jarecky was "at home," in honor of her cousin, Miss Weatherhorn, of Charleston. Progressive whist was the all absorbing game. The prize, a very handsome piece of Japanese ware, was won by Miss Ella Salley. During the progress of the games salted almonds and fine candies were served. Afterward, followed a delicious course of ice cream, cake and fruit. The parlor, in which the guests were entertained, was exquisite with choice ferns, palms and beautiful cut flowers. The intervals were filled in with music, bright and sprightly, well suited to the occasion. Miss Jarecky, who is noted for her easy, graceful manner of entertaining was well supported by Miss Mina Weatherhorn and her sister, Miss Hennie. The fortunate guests were Mrs. A. Lexia, Misses Ella Salley, Rebecque Wimberly, Edythe Loryea, Bessie Fairey, Mina Weatherhorn and Hallie Murray.

Irving and Mina made their home in NY. He started working as a lumber salesman. I have been unable to find out if he was working for the Wetherhorn family firm. Their 1910 address in NY was 500 W. 144th. That was where they were when their son Louis was born. While he was an infant they also had an 18 year old Negro servant named Clara. It almost looked like habits from the Old South were still with them. Irving soon joined the staff of United Profit Sharing Corporation and became general manager of their office at 44 W. 18th Street. The company distributed coupons through the packaging of various goods as a sales promotion aid. In a later generation many consumers saved "Green Stamps" in booklets for later redemption. The business model was very similar. The following picture shows some of the coupons issued by United Profit Sharing.

Those coupons were included in packages of soap, chewing gum, and similar consumer items. The coupons were sent by consumers

to "purchase" items in a catalog. The original manufacturer paid Irving's office for coupons that were redeemed at a rate of about $3 for every 1000 coupons. Over the period the company was active, throughout the 1920s until possibly, as late as 1950. Over a billion coupons were redeemed. The corporation, obviously, made a profit on the deal.

In any case by 1924 the Schwarz family was living at 336 28th St. in lower Manhattan, one of many apartments they rented over the years. And Irving was listed as supporting the family running a mail order hosiery business. This may have been a part of United Profit Sharing. Work was not always easy to find during the Great Depression.

By 1930 Irving had moved to another job, working in the office of a cigar company. Their son appears to have been employed at the same place. Their home was in apartment 4D of a 15 story building at 910 West End Ave. for which they paid $167 per month. The entire neighborhood was made of similar apartment houses. However, only one street away was where upper Broadway angled slightly to the West and that street was lined with the small businesses that still give that part of Manhattan its unique character.

As the great depression began to ease life improved for the Schwarz family. Irving and Mina took a winter holiday cruise vacation in 1937-8. Vacation cruises are not a new development from recent years. In 1934 there were no less than 11 special winter cruises from NY to Bermuda or Nassau and back. It was profitable enough for The Holland-America steamship line to take their passenger liner, SS STAATENDAM, off her regular trans-Atlantic runs. She made a "West Indies Holiday Cruise" departing from NY on December 18th, 1937 and returning to the same port on January 2nd, 1938. Irving and Mina were among the passengers.

I've already mentioned Louis Schwarz. I found him very difficult to follow. There were many people named Louis (or Lewis) Schwarz (or Schwartz) in New York City. Many were almost the same age. I originally picked up a 1910 US Census listing that made him an inmate in the Hebrew Orphans' Home. Only later on did I find another entry that seemed to be the correct one for him.

That record, too, led me down several blind alleys. The first WWI draft notice for Irving Schwarz was for a security guard. It was much later that I found a similar document for Irving Washington Schwarz. I know that Louis Schwarz married. I never found that he had any children. For that reason I include him in this chapter.

Louis Schwarz, the one I believe to be my cousin, married Joan Ruth Prager in NY on June 2nd, 1934. It seems the marriage was not a success because the 1940 US Census had Louis in a Chicago hotel, and indicates he was divorced. Louis married again in 1961 to Sheila Gail Peritzman, who was much younger than he. Louis died in April, 1984 in Florida. Joan R. Schwarz died in 1993 in NY, Sheila Schwarz died in NY in 1997. I am not totally sure these are the right people because Schwarz is such a common name and there is an absence of corroborating data.

Irving Washington Schwarz died in NY on May 3rd, 1946. Mina moved to Florida later in her life and died there on February 3rd 1979.

Henry Wetherhorn 1847-1901		
Spouse	**Bertha Epstein**	
Children	Sophie Wetherhorn	p. 165
	Virginia Wetherhorn	p. 165

6
HENRY WETHERHORN

Henry Wetherhorn was born in December 1847 in Charleston, South Carolina. He was the youngest of the 5 brothers born to Marcus and Zipporah. The year of his birth was also the first year the US postal service used postage stamps. The first stamps were sold in New York and came in only 2 denominations; the 5 cent red-brown picturing Benjamin Franklin, and the 10 cent black with a picture of George Washington. The amount on the black stamp was printed as "X cents". The first stamps were only in use until 1851. That year the Postal Department began issuing a new series that included other denominations and pictures, but the 10 cent stamp still used the Roman numeral "X".

When the Civil war started Henry was still too young to take an active part. He later joined The first SC Light Artillery Battery, also known as Captain Wagener's Battery Three of his older brothers were also in the same unit. He worked as a wagoner and his record also showed that he was Absent without Leave on March 24th, 1864. I found no mention of when, if ever, he returned to the unit.

When the war ended he found himself still in Charleston. The city was in ruins. He had not ben apprenticed before the war and had no profession or special skills. In need of money, he turned to criminal activity. He conspired with a Federal soldier to forge a government check. They were caught. *The Charleston Daily News* reported on September 28th, 1865 that he entered a guilty plea. Henry spent the next year in jail.

When he was released he was still faced with the same problems. He began breaking into houses to steal things. Once again, he was caught. The *Newberry Weekly Herald* reported the in results on May 23rd, 1866 in the following article:

At the Court of General Sessions, Charleston, the following sentences were pronounced:

Thos. Cook and wife Hannah Cook, convicted of larceny and sentenced—the former $200 fine, 9 months imprisonment and 10 stripes. The latter fined $100 and to receive 1 stripe.

The youths, Rantin, Smith and Wetherhorn, against whom a jury had rendered the verdict of guilty with a recommendation to mercy, were then called up to learn their doom. Although the Judge intimated that there was a hope that the clemency of the Executive would be exercised in their behalf, yet he urged upon them to place no undue reliance on this possibility, and so to dispose their minds that if their lives were to be spared their conduct would be reformed, and if their hopes should prove delusive, that they would be prepared to meet their end. The sentence of the law was, that they be carried to the place from whence they came, and there kept in safe custody until Friday, the 4th day of July next, when, between the hours of ten in the forenoon and two in the afternoon, they were to be hung by the neck until they were dead.

Until this moment the boys seemed not to appreciate the consequences of their crime; but when this awful doom was pronounced, they exhibited, by their bitter anguish, a keen realization of their perilous position.

John Rantin, J. H. L. Smith and H. Wetherhorn, all of whom are under eighteen years of age, and under the sentence of death for burglary in Charleston, have had their sentences commuted by the Governor, to hard labor in the penitentiary for the term of five years.

Perry Dunham, convicted of the murder of Thos

The Charleston Daily News.
December 29, 1866, Page 2

As noted, the Court sentenced him to death. That was a common punishment at the time for looting. Lucky for him, his youth saved him. The following article in the *Charleston Daily News* of December 29th, 1866, reports that the Governor commuted the sentences of the three teen-agers, all under eighteen, to 5 years hard labor.

This time when he was released he decided that, being known as criminal in Charleston, he ought to try starting over somewhere else. He chose Savannah, Georgia, as the location where he might begin a new life. I don't know when he first moved to Savannah, but when he did, he soon found himself welcome within the Jewish community in Savannah at the Temple Mickve Israel congregation. Rabbi Isaac Mendes of Temple Mickve Israel officiated when Henry married Bertha Epstein, age 20, on October 3rd, 1877 I liked the way the county clerk recorded the date. He made the "O" in October look like a heart.

Prior to their marriage Henry was living on Zubly Street and had found employment as a constable in the office of Justice of the Peace J. J. Abrams.

After their marriage Henry and Bertha lived with her parents in their spacious home at 51 Tattnall St. Other Epstein children also lived at the same address, including Bertha's sister, Virginia, known as Jennie, and her husband, Isaac Russell. There were 4 individuals listed as domestic servants, but one was only 10 years old.

Bertha's father, Jacob, had a wholesale grocery business. When he died in 1880 his son, Sigmund, took it over and was later in partnership with I. Berg. This was probably because the two older Epstein boys already had their own wholesale dry good business. It appears that the entire Epstein clan had moved to a new home on 191 Perry St. before Jacob Epstein died.

The 1883 Savannah City directory shows Henry still working as a county constable in the Chatham County 1st district, but now his direct employer was District Magistrate Isaac Russell, his brother-in-law. The house at

ARREST OF A GAMBLER.

Charles Bluen, Who Is Wanted in Savannah Arrested in New York.

SAVANNAH, Ga., June 23.—[Special.]—A telegram received in the city last night stated that Charles Bluen had been arrested in New York by Detective Henry Wetherhorn. Bluen was convicted in the superior court for running a gaming room, known as the "Progress Social Club." Pending sentence he was released on a $500 bond. Before sentence was passed, Bluen disappeared. It was learned that he was in New York city and Detective Wetherhorn was sent after him. Bluen was found and it is reported that for ten days Wetherhorn roomed with him, while waiting for the necessary papers to bring his man on. Governor Gordon issued a requisition, but Governor Hill of New York demanded that the proof of conviction be laid before him. That caused quite a delay. Finally everything was straightened out and Bluen was arrested. It was announced that he would be brought back to Savannah, but Captain Henry Bluen said this morning that the announcement was erroneous, and that his brother will continue to reside in New York despite the final conclusion of Governor Hill to honor Governor Gordon's requisition. Captain Bluen added:

"Justice is satisfied. I have paid the cash, and Charles Bluen will be released."

Later it was reported that Wetherhorn had left New York, on a steamer, for Savannah, with his prisoner this afternoon.

The Canadian authorities respect the word of an Englishman. The negro Adam Morse, who beat Conductor Barbee brutally, will possibly be extradited after all. Last night Solicitor General duBignon received a telegram from the crown attorney at Toronto, stating that papers had arrived and that he considered them sufficiently strong to secure an extradition on the charge of assault with intent to commit murder. While this does not definitely decide the case, as the judge of the Toronto court must pass upon the papers, it justifies sending an officer to Canada, and Detective Witherhorn will leave tonight. He will first go to Atlanta and secure the governor's requisition, and then to Washington, where the president's requisition will be obtained. He will arrive in Toronto on Sunday or Monday, giving him plenty of time to prepare for a hearing on Wednesday. Among the papers sent to the Canadian authorities, was the affidavit of Mr. Walker Robertson, British vice consul at this port, who was on the train when the alleged assault upon Morse's son took place.

191 Perry was home for Henry and Bertha's 2 daughters, and Isaac and Jennie's son. Nearby was Orleans Square, one of many lovely mini-parks with trees and grass that dotted the intersections throughout Savannah. The site of the house, however, is now the location of the Savannah Civic Center.

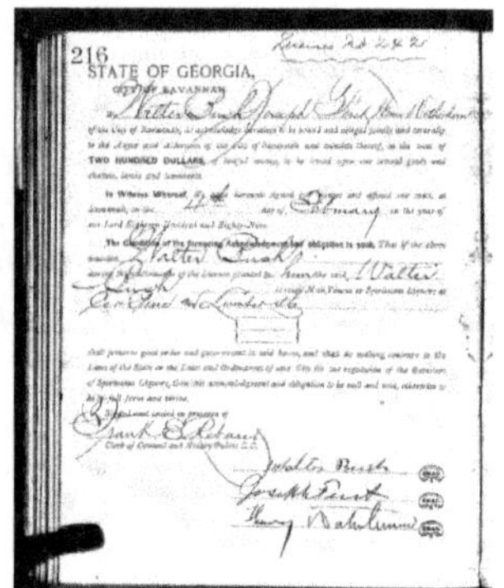

A CHILD'S PERIL.

She Is Lured Into a House of Ill Fame by a Woman.

SAVANNAH, Ga., March 25.—There is a case in the courts here that is likely to create a sensation when all of the facts are brought out, and some one will be made to suffer a severe penalty when the case is thoroughly worked up. It is in the hands of Detective Wetherhorn who rarely ever loses a point or makes a failure when he undertakes a job.

A little girl, 13 years old, was met on the street by a woman who gave her a note, asking her to take it to a well known house of ill repute. The note gave instructions that the child was to be detained in the house until its author should direct what should be done with the child. The girl remained at the house, under compulsion, four days. Meanwhile, the mother of the child was frantic with anxiety. She placed the matter in the hands of the detective. Detective Wetherhorn went to work on the case with a will.

He ascertained that the child was in charge of a woman of questionable character. The little one's hair had been cut, she had been attired in a long dress, and her appearance had been otherwise disguised. It was, it is charged, the purpose of the woman to lead the child to a life of shame. The charge of kidnapping has been placed against the women, and their prosecution will be pushed with vigor. The mother of the child will do everything in her power to bring the women to justice.

One thing that stands out in this chapter is the many newspaper reports that include mention of activities in which Henry participated. This made learning about him a very interesting and enjoyable task. This is the first report of his activities as a constable. It appeared in *The Atlanta Constitution* on June 24th, 1887

Here is another from the following year (May 18, 1882) from page 2 of *The Atlanta Constitution*). It seems Henry got to travel quite a bit while performing his duties.

I found a document dated February 4th, 1889 that showed Henry, and 2 others, were given a liquor license by the City of Savannah.

By 1891 Henry and Bertha moved a bit further south to 176 Bolton St. The large expanse of Forsyth Park was just 2 blocks away. Bertha's mother lived just down the street at 180 Bolton with her brother, Moses. Henry continued to make news. The following is part of a long report adapted from page 3 of *The Atlanta Constitution* of September 19th, 1891,

"Detectives Bedford and Crim returned from Savannah yesterday morning. They told the story of how three express robbers were traced and caught, and the capture shows up to be as fine a piece of detective work

Sternberg Denies His Suit.

Simon Sternberg, who was arrested in New York on a charge of forging the name of T. Krouskoff to a note for $750 which was discounted by the Citizens' bank, was brought back to the city today by Detective Wetherhorn, but was not taken to jail. He remained in charge of the detective until this afternoon when he gave bond for $2,000 and was released. The bank officials have refused outright to settle the case and will prosecute Sternberg to the extent of the law. He stoutly denies his guilt.

FOUR ARRESTS MADE

Of Parties Implicated in the Killing of Gibbons.

Savannah, Ga., February 16.—(Special)— Four white men were arrested today by Detectives Wetherhorn, Kiley and Scully— E. L. Guest, J. E. Connolly and D. P. Walker and Fred Floyd—for the murder of Stephen Gibbons, the negro who was shot in the hip Saturday night, in west Savannah, just after the arrival of the street car from the city.

The information that led to their arrest was given by some negroes, who were on the car at the time of the shooting. Connolly, Floyd and Walker are electric railway employes and Guest is an ex-employe of the company. They had no particular business on the car at the time of the shooting, and no business at all in west Savannah, so far as is known. They all admit being present, however, when the negro was shot.

Guest has confessed to firing the shot that proved fatal to Gibbons. He says he did the shooting in self-defense and is willing to stand all the brunt of it. He was on the car, he stated, and was in the difficulty that occurred shortly after its arrival at west Savannah. Gibbons had a revolver and was trying to shoot him, he states, when he fired upon him and wounded him in the hip. The negro shot at him at such close range, he says, that he burned his hand with the powder from the pistol.

To substantiate this statement Guest displayed his right hand, which shows some signs of a powder burn. The others in the barracks with him, Guest says, had nothing to do with the killing.

as has ever been seen in this part of the country. "I reached Savannah Saturday night" says Bedford, "and found that Crim and Basch were working on the case. The robbery only occurred the night before, but these men, and Weatherhorn, another Savannah detective, had struck a very faint trail, which, however, led to the capture of the right parties …You all know Crim, and know what good work he does.

In this case he was up to the top notch, and his work was of the very best kind. Jackson of the ex- press company is a splendid fellow, and has a long head. There few men as good anywhere. Basch is one of the shrewdest men I've struck in the business and besides knowing what to do he knows how to do it and does it…. Weatherhorn is all right, too, and with such men as these most anybody can be caught,"

The next item came from the *Polk County News* of March 10th 1892. It told of the death of Mafia leader Catillo Coumo in Savannah. The report concluded with "When he heard that Detective Wetherhorn had warrants out for him he sent around word that Wetherhorn had been put on the death list of the Mafia and that if the warrants were not

Murderer Small Taken Back.

BALTIMORE, July 24.—"Abe" Small, the colored desperado who, in Savannah, killed Policeman Neve and seriously wounded Detective Humphreys while resisting arrest, was taken last night, heavily ironed, to Savannah by Chief McDermott and Detective Wetherhorn, of that city. Small admits his identity and confesses the killing of Neve and wounding of Humphreys. The shooting, he claims, was done in self defense.

Counterfeiters Betrayed by a Negro.

SAVANNAH, May 11.—J. Frank Mason and James Morgan, counterfeiters, both white, were arrested out on the Middle Ground road about three miles from the city by Detective Wetherhorn and committed to jail by United States Commissioner Beckett. They were betrayed into the hands of the officers by a negro who had followed them from Florida.

withdrawn, Justice Naughin's name would be added to it. As to the detective himself, he proposed to kill him if he tried to serve the warrants."

Then there was this item from the Eufaula (Alabama) *Daily Times* on March 25th, 1892.

The year 1893 started with an article from The Eau Clair Wisconsin *Leader-Telegram* on January 28th.about the election of the mayor in Savannah. Detectives Wetherhorn and Basch (remember him from that earlier article?) were both mentioned.

The Atlanta Constitution on August 17th of the same year reported that Henry had been to NY to bring back another fugitive.

On May 11th, 1894 The *Pensacola News* mentioned him making yet another arrest.

And then again on July 26th, 1895 Henry shows up in the Vineland NJ *Evening Journal* for bringing a murderer back to stand trial.

The mayor's report of 1895 affirms that Henry was officially a detective, and not only a constable. The appointment dated from February 25th, 1895

On April 11th 1896 *The Atlanta Constitution* reported:

Henry also appears several times in the records of the Savannah and Chatham County Court. One of the cases from 1897 has him listed with dozens of other defendants as having been in violation of a city ordinance because they had a dog and had not reported it to the authorities. The standard penalty for most of them was a fine of $1 or 1 day in jail.

The record for November 16th, 1897 includes a section confirming his appointment as a bailiff for the court and even mentions some of his benefits and compensation in this new role.

But things weren't always so good. Henry also appears on the other side of the law. He was a defendant in a case in 1885 that was dismissed by the judge, but appeared again in July of that year charged with assault and battery. The latter case was heard first by a grand jury that decided to forward the case for trial. He was found guilty, and his attorney immediately filed a motion for a new trial even though the jury had recommended the sentence be merciful. The motion was approved, and it involved separating him from two co-defendants. At the second trial Henry admitted his guilt and was sentenced to pay $200 and spend 2 months in jail. The jail time was later dropped, but $200 was a sizable amount at that time.

This series of Newspaper and court record items shows that Henry Wetherhorn had an extremely active, and varied, professional life that also took him traveling to other places. It was quite an adventure for someone who started out as a convicted felon with a death sentence.

The Wetherhorn family, of course, remained on Bolton Street. Even though, with the passing of years the city population had already grown to about 60,000 in 1897. The city would continue to grow, but Henry would not remain for much longer.

In 1900 the extended family was living at 214 Bolton. The extended family included Henry and Bertha and their 2 daughters, as yet unmarried, plus Bertha's siblings; Abraham, Moses, and Jennie, along with Jennie's son, Robert Russell. The Epstein brothers worked as traveling salesmen and might not have been at the home much of the time.

This was the era when the next to last lynching in Chatham County occurred. Allan Brooks was accused of sexually assaulting Mrs. F. W. Hart. News of the crime spread and a vigilante group located him. A mob of some 200 people hauled him to a tree where he was hung and then many of the group emptied their revolvers into his body. When the Sheriff's men arrived all they found was his body with some 500 bullet holes. The lynch mob had evaporated and was never found.

On May 1st, 1901, Henry died from Bright's disease. Today it would probably be recorded as chronic or acute nephritis. He was buried the following day in the Hebrew section of the Laurel Grove Cemetery. He left no will. A probate hearing on May 25th ruled that Bertha inherited his estate.

By 1920 Bertha had moved to a different home at 360 W 36th Street. That year the US census takers found her presiding over a household which included her brother Abraham, her nephew Robert Russell, and her daughter Jennie plus Jennie's husband and their two sons.

Bertha suffered from diabetes and it probably contributed to her death from myocarditis, a fancy word for a heart attack, on December 19th, 1923.

Sophie Wetherhorn 1878-1910

Spouse	**Felix Meyer**

Virginia   Wetherhorn 1879-1948

Spouse	**George B Lehwald**	
Children	Henry W Lehwald	p. 168
	George B Lehwald Jr	p. 168

Sophie Wetherhorn was born in Savannah on April 1st, 1878. Her sister, Virginia was born on March 8th of the following year. Both were active in social circles.

On February 5th, 1901, when Sophie was almost 23, she was in town, walking south. She was at the corner of Macon and Abercorn on her way to catch a trolley. A man named George Thomas came up behind her. He may have been an emancipated slave, who, like her father at one time, had little income and no marketable skills. He grabbed her purse. Sophie tried to hold on, but he was stronger. She cried out "Stop. Thief!" as he ran away. Several people pursued him but lost sight of him. Another passer-by saw him hide under a stairway. An off duty fireman pulled him out of his shelter. He was still holding her purse. Thomas was taken to the police station. He claimed he had found the purse. He was charged immediately. Stealing the purse of the daughter of a detective was frowned upon. George Thomas was brought before a judge, found guilty, and sentenced to 15 years in prison. Sophie had a bruised wrist, but was otherwise unharmed. Less than a week later her father collapsed and died.

Sophie and Jennie remained at home for quite a while after their father died. Sophie married Felix Meyer, from Charleston, on June 4th, 1906. The marriage was brief. Sophie died on March 29th, 1910. She was buried the following day. She left no will, so

GOODMAN-WETHERHORN.

The marriage of Miss Jennie Wetherhorn to Mr. Ben Goodman of New York was celebrated yesterday at the home of the bride's mother, Mrs. B. Wetherhorn on Bolton street, Rev. Dr. Marx of Atlanta officiated. The bride was attended by her sister, Miss Sophie Wetherhorn, and the best man was Mr. Lou Goodman of New York.

The maid-of-honor wore a lovely gown of cream white henrietta with applique and all-over lace. She carried a bouquet of pink carnations.

The bride wore her traveling gown, a tailor suit of tan cloth, and a tan hat with pink roses under the brim and a crown of white panne velvet. Her bouquet was of white roses. A diamond sunburst, the gift of her mother, was the only ornament worn.

After the ceremony a reception was held, about 100 people being present. The house was beautifully decorated, one drawing room in white and green, the rear room and the dining room in pink and green. Among the out of town guests were Mrs. Fannie Friedman, Miss Carrie Goodman of New York; Mr. Arthur Wetherhorn of Waynesboro, and Mr. Mortimer Jarecky of St. Matthews, S. C.

Mr. and Mrs. Goodman left almost immediately, after the ceremony for New York, their future home, where Mr. Goodman holds the position of general salesman for C. B. Rouss.

her husband and uncle, Abram Epstein, paid $600 for a probate that settled all her estate on Felix. They had no children. There are many people named Felix Meyer, and I was unable to follow his life after she died with any certainty whatsoever.

Virginia was almost always known as Jennie. She should not be confused with her maternal aunt, Virginia Epstein Russel, who was also known as Jennie. There were times when the two Jennies both lived in the same home. The Wetherhorn family of Savannah was well known. Jennie and her sister Sophie were no strangers to the society column of the *Savannah Daily News.* One of the bigger stories in the paper on the last day of 1902 was the marriage of Jennie to Benjamin Goodman of New York. The ceremony took place at her home and was conducted by the Reverend Dr. David Marx of the Atlanta Reform temple. Sophie was maid of honor. Sadly, the marriage was not a success. Very brief announcement in the same paper on November 26th, 1904 said that a divorce had been filed for and that Jennie would be asking to have her maiden name restored. The latter announcement contained only 9 short lines.

Jennie had remained at home with her mother when Sophie and Felix moved to their own home at 1 Duffy Street. Jennie was well into her thirties when she finally married George B. Lehwald, who was 5 years older than she, on August 13th, 1913 in the Mickve Israel chapel in Savannah.

The couple lived at 307 36th Street, West. By 1920 her widowed mother and her unmarried uncle, Abraham, were also living with them, along with her Aunt Jennie's grandsons,

Robert and Joseph Russell. At that time they also employed two black female servants. Jennie and George remained in the Epstein family home on Bolton and soon had two sons, Henry and George Jr. Their father ran his own business. His Grand Billiard Parlor was located at 17-19 Congress Street opposite Johnson Square, one of the oldest of Savannah's lovely little parks. When America joined the First World War George registered for the draft. He was already 44 years old and had 2 small children. The Army did not call on him

In 1927 the city directory showed that George had given up on the pool halls and was now working as the superintendent of the city garage. His timing in leaving the billiards business was probably very good. Pool halls were very popular in the early part of the 20th century. It has been said that there as many as 800 of them in Chicago alone, before the First World War. After WW II the fact that they sold alcoholic beverages caused a public reaction and many locales passed city ordinances or laws prohibiting minors from entering them. The 1930 census indicated that the Lehwalds owned the home at 307 36th Street. That was probably a great help when the country descended into the depths of the great depression. The census also showed Jennie's uncle Abram still living with them, along with her cousin Robert Russell and his son, Robert Jr. They even still had a Negro maid. All of the relatives were gainfully employed and I assume they also contributed financially.

A decade later none of the relatives remained. George was still fully employed and earning $1300 a year. Both sons were still at home, unmarried. Henry, the older boy, was bringing home $800 a year as a shoe store salesman. It's likely that he was working at his Uncle Samuel Lehwald's shoe store. His father had also worked for another, older, brother before he married. The Lehwalds also took in a boarder, both because they had space and to help provide extra income.

Jennie died on May 18th, 1948 and was buried the following day in Lot 1722 of the Hebrew section of Laurel Grove Cemetery.

George died on July 28th 1955 and was laid to rest alongside his wife in lot 1723.

Henry W Lehwald
1915-1989

Spouse	**Gertrude Stokes**
Children	Dolores Lehwald
	Henry W Lehwald Jr

George B Lehwald Jr
1917-1953

Spouse	**Nell Malette**
Children	Paul Lamar Lehwald

Henry Wetherhorn Lehwald was born in Savannah, Georgia, on December 19th, 1915. His brother George B. Lehwald Jr. was born in October of 1917.When he was still young George Jr. was infected by Polio. He survived, but was left with one arm and one leg crippled.

They both grew up in their grandmother's house on 36th Street. Both boys had grey eyes and brown hair. Henry was nicknamed Mutt. He was employed at his Uncle Max's clothing store at 114 E. Broughton. George, nicknamed Butch, eventually was employed at an NVC project at the Savannah fairgrounds.

This is the point where our time frame runs out. But I do want to add that Henry was 5'10" tall and weighed 172 pounds in 1940, and he met Gertrude Stokes, usually known as Bobbie. Bobbie had been married, officially, in 1937, to a man named Allen B. Crawford. I never found a record of a divorce or annulment, but Mr. Crawford married again, to someone else, three years later. Henry and Bobbie were joined in matrimony on January 24th, 1941.

Butch eventually married Nell Mallette. They even had a son. But George W. Lehwald Jr. died on May 8th, 1953 at the age of 33.

Henry Wetherhorn 1847-1901

Henry raised 2 children and finally died on December 31st, 1989.

There is a Lehwald section in Laurel Hill Cemetery in Savannah where they are both buried, Gertrude Stokes is there under the Hebrew name "Ruth Bat Abraham" That name, and the location of her grave, indicates that she was probably converted to Judaism.

Sigmund M Wetherhorn
1858-1891

Spouse	Esther Rubinstein
Children	Fannie Wetherhorn

7
Sigmund Wetherhorn

Sigmund Wetherhorn was born in Charleston on February 14th 1858 One of the oldest family photos I have is of him, in the center, with his sister, Anne, and brother, Solomon. It was taken about 1868

Charleston schools, at that time, were all free. There were 3 white schools and 1 colored school in the system with 46 teachers and 3171 pupils listed for the white schools. The schools in the city were regarded locally as among the best in the South, and possibly in the entire nation. St. Philips, where Sigmund was

enrolled, had a primary section with 12 classes, an intermediate level with 6 classes, and a 'boy's grammar department' that contained another 6 classes. On April 1st, 1870 The *Charleston Daily News* carried a list of the star pupils. It was called the city examination awards list. Sigmund was in the intermediate level at St. Philips School. He was in the third class and received the First Premium award.

In 1880, When Sigmund was 22; he lived in St. Matthews with his widowed mother and his siblings. He opened his own shop where he sold liquor and cigars. Social life for many Jews in the South was centered on the Jewish holidays. In 1886 a number of families got together and organized a masked ball to celebrate the Purim holiday. The event got extended coverage in the local

Orangeburg *Times and Democrat* newspaper. There was mention of the venue, the band, and an extensive list of the participants, including their costumes. Both Sigmund and his brother Solomon were mentioned, and they both came as bootblacks.

The 1890 Purim Ball got similar treatment in the same paper. This time Sol came as Black Jack, and Annie as Queen of the Night. Sigmund wasn't mentioned separately, but the article did note that Mrs. S. M. Wetherhorn was present, but not masked. From this I surmised that Sigmund had already married Esther Rubinstein from Augusta Georgia. The couple had a daughter, name Fannie, in 1891. The child never really got to know her father. Sigmund became ill and died after 6 days from Uremia. Esther was then 34 years old. She took her daughter and moved to Georgia to live with her mother.

I believe that her mother, Frances Asher Rubinstein, who ran a confectionery in Savannah, was aware that the assistant sexton of the synagogue had recently lost his wife and had a number of children who were now motherless. Connections were made somehow, and Esther Wetherhorn married Samuel Jacobs in 1898. Little Fannie now had a stepfather. She kept her biological father's name until she married John Thomas Garret in 1925. I am not aware of them ever having children. By 1940 Fannie was a widow living in a house in Richmond for which she paid $30 a month rent. She worked as a bookkeeper for a hospital and earned $900 a year. Her next door neighbor was the administrator of the hospital.

Sigmund had died without leaving a will. Not surprising, since he had passed away so young. Isadore Pinkussohn was appointed by the probate court to settle the estate. There were two mandatory notices in the newspapers asking for anyone with claims to come forward followed by two more that announced the date the remaining stock at the liquor and cigar store would be sold at public auction. Sigmund had been buried long before that happened.

Solomon, the younger boy in the photograph, was born in Charleston on December 7th, 1862. At the turn of the century census he was listed living with his widowed mother at the home of his sister Annie. He worked as a clerk in a general store, and later joined his brother-in-law in the cotton trade.

He was reported as having contributed much to building up St. Matthews, but, as far as I know, he never married. He died on Sunday morning, September 30th, 1906 in St Matthews.

David, the youngest sibling, who doesn't appear in the photograph, was born on August 16th, 1864. He appears to have moved about. In 1886 he was living in Savannah, GA. That was the same year that the US Army brought 75 Apache Indians from Arizona to be held in a Federal encampment in St. Augustine, Fl. It's easy to forget that the United States was embarked on a series of "wars" with various Indian tribes in the decade immediately following the Civil War. Those campaigns almost invariably brought ruin to the American Indian tribes. The following year, 1887, found David in Ocala. FL. But he was back in South Carolina when he died on December 3rd, 1899. He, too, never married.

Annie Wetherhorn
1861-1913

Spouse   Morris Jarecky

Children   Mortimer M Jarecky

Albert Henry Jarecky

Pauline Jarecky

Henriette W Jarecky

Sigmund Jarecky

8
Annie Wetherhorn Jarecky

Annie Wetherhorn was born on July 7th 1862. She was only 18 when she married Morris Jarecky in St Matthews on November 3rd, 1880. Morris was almost 14 years older than she. But it turned out well. He had come from Germany in 1864 and found a business opportunity in St Matthews. Morris made a good living as a merchant. The local paper described his situation in 1891 in the following clipping:

The couple raised 4 children whose stories appear in their own brief chapters. A fifth child, Sigmund Jarecky, was born on April 15th, 1898. He survived only about 2 months.

> M. Jarecky, who is one of the enterprising merchants here, does a large and extensive trade in groceries, plantation supplies, dry goods, hardware, furniture, shoes, hats, and caps. His store occupies a space twenty feet long and twenty-five feet wide.

In 1910 the Jareckys lived very close to Sheppard and Sarah Pearlstine in St. Matthews. The older Pearlstine son would, in future, marry my Aunt, Sophie Zerline Wetherhorn. But at the time they were also joined by a common tragedy of having lost a child at an early age. The Pearlstine's' son, Nathan, was born on August 13th, 1906. He had serious indigestion problems. His father's cousin, Dr. Kivvy Pearlstine, had been treating him for two years before he died on November 15th, 1909. He was only 3 years, 3 months, and 2 days old.

On Saturday, August 11th, 1911 *The Times and Democrat* described an experience that was probably quite common in the early days of automobiles.

> At St. Matthews one day last week the horse of Mr. M. Jarecky took fright at an automobile and turned the buggy over, throwing him and his little grand daughter out. Luckily they escaped unhurt.

Morris Jarecky.

Special to The State.

St. Matthews, March 2.—Morris Jarecky, one of the oldest and most highly esteemed citizens of St. Matthews died at the home of his daughter, Mrs. Archie Stiener, in Richmond, Va., today at 11 o'clock. Mr. Jarecky had been in failing health for some years. No appreciable decline manifested itself, however, until the death of his wife in 1913, after which he seemed less concerned in the matters of this life and often expressed a desire to join his departed loved one. Born in a Prussian province 70 years ago, he came to this country in 1868. He landed at New York and from there came immediately to Charleston. After a stay of three months in Charleston, he came to St. Matthews (then Lewisville) and had ever since made this his home. He went into the mercantile business at once and his business still stands today as he organized it. It was always one of his proudest sayings that he had been in business all these years and never paid an account with less than 100 cents on the dollar. When he arrived here, he had $2. Today his estate is one of the handsomest in this section of the country. Of the kindliest and most happy disposition he was loved by all and the children always found him ready for a romp. Customers traded with him for years. His liberality was one of his shining marks. He gave to all alike and although of the orthodox Jewish faith, he counted himself slighted if any church or solicitor for charity overlooked him. In 1880 he was married to Miss Annie Weatherhorn. She died in 1913. To this marriage were born four children, Mrs. Archie Stiner of Richmond, Va., and Miss Hennie Jarecky of this place. M. M. Jarecky, who now has charge of the mercantile business here, and Lieut. Albert Jarecky of the National Army. A brother, Leopold Jarecky, and a sister, Mrs. Fannie Flanders of New York, also survive him. The remains will be interred tomorrow at 12 o'clock at the Jewish Cemetery at Orangeburg.

Annie lived to see her remaining children wed and raising their own families. On Sunday afternoon, January 19th, 1913, she was not feeling well. In less than half an hour later she was dead. The local paper, *The Times and Democrat*, had this to say about her.

"Mrs. Jarecky was Miss Annie Weatherhorn of Charleston and was 51 years old. She was married to Morris Jarecky 31 years ago and since that time has made her home here, being in a large measure responsible for establishing the high tone of womanly energy and beautiful simplicity which characterizes the social world here."

Morris survived her by only 2 years.

Mortimer M Jarecky
1881-1931

Spouse   Ruth Henrietta Kahn

Albert Henry Jarecky
1888-1964

Spouse   Rena May Welsh

Mortimer Matthew Jarecky was born in Charleston on the last day of August, 1881. He had brown eyes and black hair and he grew up to be a bit shorter, and much stockier than his brother Albert. The two were quite close throughout their lives.

Morty studied to be a lawyer, but spent his earlier years helping his father in the family store.

Mortimer married Ruth Henrietta Kahn in Charleston on February 13th, 1913. He was already 32 and she was barely 20.

Ruth was the youngest of 12 children of Jules and Mina Kahn, Her sister, Rosalie, who was 20 years older, was the wife of Leopold Wetherhorn, Technically, that made Ruth the aunt of my father and his siblings, even though according to her age, she was more a contemporary. My father always called her "Aunt Ruth", but they were all very close in both age and relationships. I have a couple of pictures of her with my cousin, Elaine Pearlstine, they show how

short Ruth was, and also confirm that she had learned to play the piano. The Piano picture is dated June 1943.

Ruth and Mortimer never had children. They spent a few years in Augusta Georgia, where his brother Albert had set up a cotton trading business. In 1925 Albert's office was at 735 Reynolds in Augusta and Albert and his wife, Rena, lived at 2339 Kingsway. Mortimer and Ruth lived at 1436 Jones Road and his law office was at room 312 in the 16 story high Lamar Building, renamed the Southern Finance Building in 1925. That structure was a center for law offices. In 1929 at least 35 lawyers had offices there. The Chamber of Commerce had their office on the ground floor of the Lamar Building. Many other law offices were located in buildings along the 700 block on Broad Street. Besides the Lamar Building at 753 there was the Marion Building at 729, slightly smaller, being only 10 stories high. Then there were the 5 story Leonard Building at 702 and the 4 story Herald Building at 725. Together they were home to most of the law offices in the city at that time. The Herald Building is particularly interesting because it is home to the city's newspapers. Originally built for the *Augusta Herald,* it also

housed the *Augusta Chronicle.* The two papers merged after the era covered here.

But I've gotten ahead of the story a bit. Albert Henry Jarecky was born on March 17th, 1888, in St Matthews. He was 29 years old when he registered for the draft in World War One. The Army accepted him for service and sent him off to be an officer in the Quartermasters Corps. Albert received his commission as a second lieutenant on August 15th, 1917. He was promoted to 1st lieutenant on March 16th, 1918. He spent the entire war at several different camps in the United States.

He never went overseas. Albert married Rena May Welsh, who was some 7 years younger, on November 1st, 1924. They took up residence in Augusta, where his older brother had also moved. Albert and Rena also remained childless.

A.H. Jarecky & Co., with offices at 735 Reynolds, was Albert's headquarters for dealing in cotton. It was just a block away from Broad and around the corner from the Augusta Cotton Exchange on 8th Street. It was also just a block away from the Savannah River that marks the boundary between Georgia and South Carolina.

On June 4th, when in Columbia, SC, Mortimer suffered a fatal heart attack. He was just 45 years old. His body was taken to Orangeburg, SC, for burial. Ruth never remarried. She later moved to Raleigh, NC, where she managed a little women's clothing store called the Betty Gay Shop on Fayetteville Street, between Marilyn Shoes and Jolly's Jewelers. She died in May, 1979.

Albert and Rena lived a quiet and comfortable life until well after the end of the period covered in this book.

Albert died at home on December 11th, 1964. He was buried in Orangeburg; SC. Rena survived until September 30th, 1988. She was interred along side her husband in plot A18 of the Orangeburg Sunnyside Cemetery.

This picture dates from 1947 and shows Ruth Jarecky on the left with Sophie Zerline Wetherhorn Pearlstine in the center and Mildred Wetherhorn Gandler on the right.

Pauline Jarecky	
1884- 1928	
Spouse	**Archie Irvin Steiner**
Children	June Ann Steiner
	Solomon A Steiner

Henrietta   Jarecky
1890-1959

An At Home.

At St. Matthews on Tuesday afternoon of last week from 4.30 to 7.30 o'clock Miss Pauline Jarecky was "at home," in honor of her cousin, Miss Weatherhorn, of Charleston. Progressive whist was the all absorbing game. The prize, a very handsome piece of Japanese ware, was won by Miss Ella Salley. During the progress of the games salted almonds and fine candies were served. Afterward, followed a delicious course of ice cream, cake and fruit. The parlor, in which the guests were entertained, was exquisite with choice ferns, palms and beautiful cut flowers. The intervals were filled in with music, bright and sprightly, well suited to the occasion. Miss Jarecky, who is noted for her easy, graceful manner of entertaining was well supported by Miss Mina Weatherhorn and her sister, Miss Hennie. The fortunate guests were Mrs. A. Lesia, Misses Ella Salley, Rebecque Wimberly, Edythe Loryea, Bessie Fairey, Mina Weatherhorn and Hallie Murray.

Pauline Jarecky was born on July 17th, 1884 in St. Matthews, SC. That was where she grew up.

The Wetherhorn and Jarecky families were part of the Society scene in the region at the time. This news item appeared in the *Times and Democrat* on June 28th, 1905 and is an indication of that standing.

This newspaper clip also bears witness to the close relations between the cousins in the same age groups. In 1905 Pauline was 21, Her sister Henrietta was nearing 16, and

Hermina Wetherhorn was 20.

The extended family relations also show up in the report on Pauline's wedding. The article originally appeared in *The American Israelite* on June 25th, 1908. The paper was published in Cincinnati, Ohio, but covered Jewish news from all over the country. The wedding actually took place on June 10th. The Wald, Link, Marcus, and Rich families, who are all mentioned as among the guests, were members of the extended Wetherhorn family through various marriages.

Pauline and her husband, Archie Steiner, would settle in his hometown of Richmond, Virginia, where he and his brother Sam ran both a shoe store, at 120 E. Broad Street, and a pawnbrokers shop, at 1441 E. Main. The latter was sometimes referred to as a loan agency. At the time of the wedding Archie was 27 years old. He had brown hair, brown eyes, and was a little on the heavy side.

St. Matthews, S. C.—The marriage of Miss Pauline Jarecky, of this place, to Mr. Archie Irvin Steiner, of Richmond, Va., was solemnized June 10th, at the home of the bride's parents, Mr. and Mrs. Morris Jarecky, the Rev. Dr. B. Elzas, of Charleston, S. C., officiating. The bride being a social belle, this marriage was looked forward to with much anticipation. Mrs. Steiner numbers her friends by the score. She has scattered sunshine and happiness in her every path, always extending a helping hand at any time and being exceedingly talented she has contributed muchly to the social life of her town. Mr. Steiner is a young man of sterling worth and very popular in his native home. The couple's popularity was greatly attested by the numerous and valuable presents, cablegrams and telegrams which they received. Among the out-of-town guests were: Mr. and Mrs. Levi Wetherhorn, Charleston, S. C.; Mr. and Mrs. B. Kahnweiler, Mr. and Mrs. Sol Kohn, Miss Kohn, Miss Henrietta Kohn, Mrs. Victor Wald, Misses Wald, Mr. Louis Link, Mr. Sol Link, Miss Marcus, Mr. and Mrs. Philip Rich and family, all of Orangeburg, S. C.; Mr. and Mrs. Sigmund Zacharias, Mr. Stahl, of Atlanta, Ga.; Mr. and Mrs. I. Rich, Miss Rosa Rich, Mr. Simon Rich, of Blackville, S. C.

The Steiners had two children, both of whom have their own chapters. Both were born while Archie and Pauline lived in Richmond. At some point, Archie decided to get out of private business and took a job as a claims agent for the Chesapeake and Ohio Railroad. They set him up in an office in Huntington, West Virginia. They were there in 1925, and maybe even earlier. Around 1928, when Pauline died, Huntington had a population of almost 80,000.

To put things in perspective, Denver Colorado had 235,000 residents that same year.

Pauline's sister, Henrietta, did not leave much of mark behind. She was born on January 6th, 1890, in St Matthews, SC. I linked the Jarecky brothers in the previous chapter. The sisters appear to have been even closer. But Hennie never married. In the 1920 US Census she showed up at the Steiner home in Richmond. At first, I thought she might just have been visiting. There was no profession listed, and Pauline must have certainly had room for her. In 1920 the Steiners even employed a mulatto house maid named Hattie Nelson. But it seems she was to become a regular member of the family. By May, 1928, she was listed as Hannah Jarecky in the Huntington West Virginia Directory as a saleswoman at the Princess Shop, and living with the Steiners. She remained with Archie after Pauline died in 1928,

Pauline was just shy of her 44th birthday when she had a "Subpial Hemorrhage". That's a fancy medical term for a stroke caused by bleeding inside the brain.

Henrietta and Archie were in Huntington until 1937. That was the year a tragic natural disaster struck the town. Huntington was situated on the Ohio River. January of 1937 was warmer than normal. The river was half a mile wide as it came past Huntington and the Ohio River dams were expected to keep it at a depth of about 9 feet. But then came 19 straight days of heavy rain and snow. The river rose to over 17 feet above flood level in Huntington. On the previous page is a picture of the Princess Shop where Henrietta had worked.

After the flood Archie and Henrietta relocated to Chicago. They were not there for long. Archie died in Chicago on November 29th 1940. His body was sent to Orangeburg, SC where he was buried alongside his wife.

Henrietta left Chicago and went to Pomona, California. She died there on September 18th, 1959.

June Ann Steiner
1909-1969

Spouse	**Wilbur Forest Moore**
Spouse	**J McClelland**
Children	Patricia J McClelland

June Ann Steiner was born on June 15th, 1909 in Richmond, Virginia. She went to High School in Huntington, WVA and graduated with the June 1926 class. At the school she was known as a smart dresser. In fact, she was quoted as saying "As good be out of the world as out of fashion." She wore her hair short, as was the style in the era of the roaring twenties. This is her graduation picture.

The picture listed her as "June", but at home they called her "Annie". On October 5th, 1933 she married Joseph B. McClelland. He was Huntington native that had gone away to Lewisburg, to the Greenbrier Military School for High School. Greenbrier, at that time, was the oldest private military school in the US. It closed in 1931. By that time McClelland was in Poughkeepsie NY at the Eastman College for Salesmen. That school, also known as the Eastman Business College, taught subjects like shorthand, accounting, penmanship, and telegraph using a "learn by doing", hands on approach. The marriage did not last long. They had a daughter, Patricia Joanne, in September 1934 and divorce soon followed. By April, 1940, June had taken her little girl with her and was living with her father and brother and Aunt Henrietta in Chicago

June had better luck with a second marriage to Wilber Forest Moore in 1942. Ultimately, June Anne died on June 3rd 1969 in Pomona CA. the same city where her Aunt had gone.

Solomon Alvin Steiner
1917-1982

Spouse   **Marie Jesse Cole**

Children   Paul Albert Steiner

Solomon Alvin Steiner was born on January 10th, 1917 in Richmond, VA. He almost never used his first name. He preferred to be known as Alvin Steiner. He enrolled in the liberal arts program at Northwestern University with an eye toward continuing on to medical school. But then World War II intervened. After the war Alvin married Marie Jesse Cole. They raised 2 children. Alvin died on February 26th, 1982 in California.

9
Those Left Behind

When I was growing up and I first heard about The Holocaust it had no personal connection for me. After all, I was a 5th generation American. My great Grandfather served with the Confederate forces in the Civil War. I had no idea that there were cousins, albeit distant, that remained in Germany when my great great grandfather left for America.

When I was in University I ran across the transcripts from the Nurnberg trials of the Nazi leaders, I read almost all of them. I was appalled at the inhumanity. But it still had no direct connection to me, personally.

When I began studying genealogy, I did not find any other family connections at first. Later on I discovered that my great great grandfather had siblings that remained in Germany. They had families, too. When the Nazis came to power, many of them managed to leave Germany. They went to many different places; South Africa, Palestine, Argentina, England, and America. But there were others that did not escape.

This is just a list of my relatives that I know were victims of the Nazi horrors.

Louis Bauer	1872-1944	Auschwitz
Klara Stern Bauer	1872-1944	Auschwitz
Berthold Bauer	1905-1943	Treblinka
Betty Seigbert Bauer	1906-1943	Treblinka
Rikchen Strauss Bauer	1886-1943	Sobibor
Mathilde Wetterhahn Jonas	1871- 1942	Auschwitz
Karl Katz	1874-1944	Auschwitz
Katinka Wetterhahn Katz	1876-1944	Auschwitz
Arthur Rosenthal	1904-1942	Terezin
Erna Katz Rosenthal	1906-1942	Auschwitz

Ruthi Rosenthal	1934-1943	Auschwitz
Lina Rosenthal	1885-1945	Treblinka
Adolf Karbe	1911-1945	Treblinka
Elsa Rosenthal Karbe	1911-1945	Treblinka
Renate Karbe	1936-1945	Treblinka
Recha Karbe	1940-1945	Treblinka
Zilla Karbe	1941-1945	Treblinka
Siegfried Rosenthal	1913-1945	Treblinka
Thekla Metzger Rosenthal	1908-1945	Treblinka
Martin Rosenthal	1919-1945	Treblinka
Karl Kohlhagen	1880-1941	Minsk
Rosa Strauss Kohlhagen	1881-1943	?

There may be others like myself that think they were untouched by the Holocaust. Like me, they are mistaken. It touched on all Jews, everywhere, because those victims were all part of our greater family. We should never forget them.

10
Over Hills and Mountains

In the Introduction I mentioned that I encountered problems with the family name. Wetherhorn is NOT a common name. It should have been, and often was, easy to locate information. But my own experience had taught me that people don't always spell a name correctly. They write what they think they heard, even when you spell it out for them. Here are some of the various ways that the family name was, or might have been, spelled: Wetherhorn, Wetterhahn, Vetterhahn, Wetherhahn, Witherhorn, Weatherhorn, Whetherhorn, Weatherhour, Detherhorn, Witterhorn, Weatherhorne, and Vetterhorn. Given names also have variations. This is especially true for those of the family who continued to follow the Jewish religion. Many had Hebrew names as well as English names. Add to that the nicknames and diminutives and the numbers of variations to be looked at becomes very large.

Jewish cemeteries mark graves in Hebrew with the patronymic form of the name, Avraham Ben Shmuel. That would be Abraham the son of Samuel in English. Many other cultures use the same form. Family names are even developed from it, like Johnson or Ericsson. In Russia or Slavic countries they use names like Mikhaelovitch or Mikhaelovna. Central Asian Georgia, as opposed to the American State of the same name, uses Gregorashvili. In Iceland there aren't even any fixed family names. Everyone is identified by a patronymic. Land ownership records in the old Ottoman Turkish Empire were recorded as belonging to Abd al Rahman bin Ibrahim. But when his grandson sold the same plot of land the names were totally different. Research into those records means you must also be a genealogist. Tracing male descendants is relatively easy. But the girls take on the name of their husband. It can become complicated.

I mentioned that Wetherhorn was/is not a common name, regardless of how it is spelled. My father once won a bet when he was living in New York City. He said there would not be another Wetherhorn using our spelling of the name in the entire NYC phone book. He included all 5 boroughs. At the time there were al- ready a couple of million people living in the city. He won the bet.

My wife often says if anyone were to run across a Wetherhorn they are probably our relatives. But searching for variant spellings can have interesting results. I found Marva Weatherhorn that way. She isn't related. But she is a beautiful young woman who was selected as Miss Guatemala in 2004!

When I was working in Zurich, Switzerland I found a mountain nearby named the Wetterhorn. Many Swiss family names come from the area where they lived. I checked the registry of Swiss family names that goes back several centuries. Wetterhorn was NOT there. By the way, there is a mountain in Colorado that is also called the Wetterhorn. It takes its name from the Swiss mountain.

I found a location in England called Wetherhorn Hill. Nobody lives there, and, as far as I have been able to determine, the name was never used to define a family.

That leaves the German story. Wetterhahn in German means a Weathercock. When the local duke required that the Jewish residents of several small villages take family names, one family became Wetterhahn because theirs was the only house to have such an ornament on the roof.